Investment Lawyer's Reference Guide: Securities Act of 1933

as amended through P.L. 115–174, enacted May 24, 2018

This Publication is designed to provide accurate and authoritative information in regard to the subject matter covered. It is sold with the understanding that the Publisher is not engaged in rendering legal, accounting, or other professional service. If legal advice or other expert assistance is required, the services of a competent professional should be sought.

Nothing contained herein is intended or written to be used for the purposes of (1) avoiding penalties imposed under the federal Internal Revenue Code, or (2) promoting, marketing, or recommending to another party any transaction or matter addressed herein.

No copyright claim is made to original government works.

A Note to Users:

This publication does not represent an official version of any Federal law and should not be cited as legal evidence of the law. It is designed to serve as a reference aid, compiling updated versions of certain key statutes as maintained by the Office of the Legislative Counsel of the United States Congress.

The official version of Federal law is found in the United States Statutes at Large and in the United States Code (*available at* http://uscode.house.gov). Before relying solely on the contents of this publication, such official versions should be consulted and appropriate professional advice should be sought.

This publication has a cut off date of June 12, 2019.

SECURITIES ACT OF 1933

[References in brackets **[ ]** are to title 15, United States Code]

[As Amended Through P.L. 115–174, Enacted May 24, 2018]

[Currency: This publication is a compilation of the text of Chapter 38 of the 73rd Congress. It was last amended by the public law listed in the As Amended Through note above and reflects current law through the date of the enactment of the public law listed at https://www.govinfo.gov/app/collection/comps/]

[Note: While this publication does not represent an official version of any Federal statute, substantial efforts have been made to ensure the accuracy of its contents. The official version of Federal law is found in the United States Statutes at Large and in the United States Code. The legal effect to be given to the Statutes at Large and the United States Code is established by statute (1 U.S.C. 112, 204).]

AN ACT To provide full and fair disclosure of the character of securities sold in interstate and foreign commerce and through the mails, and to prevent frauds in the sale thereof, and for other purposes.

Be it enacted by the Senate and House of Representatives of the United States of America in Congress assembled,

TITLE I

SHORT TITLE

SECTION 1. **[77a]** This title may be cited as the "Securities Act of 1933".

DEFINITIONS

SEC. 2. **[77b]** (a) DEFINITIONS.—When used in this title, unless the context otherwise requires—

(1) The term "security" means any note, stock, treasury stock, security future, security-based swap, bond, debenture, evidence of indebtedness, certificate of interest or participation in any profit-sharing agreement, collateral-trust certificate, preorganization certificate or subscription, transferable share, investment contract, voting-trust certificate, certificate of deposit for a security, fractional undivided interest in oil, gas, or other mineral rights, any put, call, straddle, option, or privilege on any security, certificate of deposit, or group or index of securities (including any interest therein or based on the value thereof), or any put, call, straddle, option, or privilege entered into on a national securities exchange relating to foreign currency, or, in general, any interest or instrument commonly known as a "security", or any certificate of interest or participation in, temporary or interim certificate for, receipt for, guar-

antee of, or warrant or right to subscribe to or purchase, any of the foregoing.

(2) The term "person" means an individual, a corporation, a partnership, an association, a joint-stock company, a trust, any unincorporated organization, or a government or political subdivision thereof. As used in this paragraph the term "trust" shall include only a trust where the interest or interests of the beneficiary or beneficiaries are evidenced by a security.

(3) The term "sale" or "sell" shall include every contract of sale or disposition of a security or interest in a security, for value. The term "offer to sell", "offer for sale", or "offer" shall include every attempt or offer to dispose of, or solicitation of an offer to buy, a security or interest in a security, for value. The terms defined in this paragraph and the term "offer to buy" as used in subsection (c) of section 5 shall not include preliminary negotiations or agreements between an issuer (or any person directly or indirectly controlling or controlled by an issuer, or under direct or indirect common control with an issuer) and any underwriter or among underwriters who are or are to be in privity of contract with an issuer (or any person directly or indirectly controlling or controlled by an issuer, or under direct or indirect common control with an issuer). Any security given or delivered with, or as a bonus on account of, any purchase of securities or any other thing, shall be conclusively presumed to constitute a part of the subject of such purchase and to have been offered and sold for value. The issue or transfer of a right or privilege, when originally issued or transferred with a security, giving the holder of such security the right to convert such security into another security of the same issuer or of another person, or giving a right to subscribe to another security of the same issuer or of another person, which right cannot be exercised until some future date, shall not be deemed to be an offer or sale of such other security; but the issue or transfer of such other security upon the exercise of such right of conversion or subscription shall be deemed a sale of such other security. Any offer or sale of a security futures product by or on behalf of the issuer of the securities underlying the security futures product, an affiliate of the issuer, or an underwriter, shall constitute a contract for sale of, sale of, offer for sale, or offer to sell the underlying securities. Any offer or sale of a security-based swap by or on behalf of the issuer of the securities upon which such security-based swap is based or is referenced, an affiliate of the issuer, or an underwriter, shall constitute a contract for sale of, sale of, offer for sale, or offer to sell such securities. The publication or distribution by a broker or dealer of a research report about an emerging growth company that is the subject of a proposed public offering of the common equity securities of such emerging growth company pursuant to a registration statement that the issuer proposes to file, or has filed, or that is effective shall be deemed for purposes of paragraph (10) of this subsection and section 5(c) not to constitute an offer for sale or offer to sell a security, even if the broker or dealer is participating or will participate in the registered offering of the securities of the

issuer. As used in this paragraph, the term "research report" means a written, electronic, or oral communication that includes information, opinions, or recommendations with respect to securities of an issuer or an analysis of a security or an issuer, whether or not it provides information reasonably sufficient upon which to base an investment decision.

(4) The term "issuer" means every person who issues or proposes to issue any security; except that with respect to certificates of deposit, voting-trust certificates, or collateral-trust certificates, or with respect to certificates of interest or shares in an unincorporated investment trust not having a board of directors (or persons performing similar functions) or of the fixed, restricted management, or unit type, the term "issuer" means the person or persons performing the acts and assuming the duties of depositor or manager pursuant to the provisions of the trust or other agreement or instrument under which such securities are issued; except that in the case of an unincorporated association which provides by its articles for limited liability of any or all of its members, or in the case of a trust, committee, or other legal entity, the trustees or members thereof shall not be individually liable as issuers of any security issued by the association, trust, committee, or other legal entity; except that with respect to equipment-trust certificates or like securities, the term "issuer" means the person by whom the equipment or property is or is to be used; and except that with respect to fractional undivided interests in oil, gas, or other mineral rights, the term "issuer" means the owner of any such right or of any interest in such right (whether whole or fractional) who creates fractional interests therein for the purpose of public offering.

(5) The term "Commission" means the Securities and Exchange Commission.

(6) The term "Territory" means Puerto Rico, the Virgin Islands, and the insular possessions of the United States.[1]

(7) The term "interstate commerce" means trade or commerce in securities or any transportation or communication relating thereto among the several States or between the District of Columbia or any Territory of the United States and any State or other Territory, or between any foreign country and any State, Territory, or the District of Columbia, or within the District of Columbia.

(8) The term "registration statement" means the statement provided for in section 6, and includes any amendment thereto and any report, document, or memorandum filed as part of such statement or incorporated therein by reference.

(9) The term "write" or "written" shall include printed, lithographed, or any means of graphic communication.

(10) The term "prospectus" means any prospectus, notice, circular, advertisement, letter, or communication, written or by radio or television, which offers any security for sale or confirms the sale of any security; except that (a) a communication

---

[1] The words "Philippine Islands" were deleted from the definition of the term "Territory" on the basis of Presidential Proclamation No. 2695, effective July 4, 1946 (11 F.R. 7517; 60 Stat. 1352), which granted independence to the Philippine Islands.

sent or given after the effective date of the registration statement (other than a prospectus permitted under subsection (b) of section 10) shall not be deemed a prospectus if it is proved that prior to or at the same time with such communication a written prospectus meeting the requirements of subsection (a) of section 10 at the time of such communication was sent or given to the person to whom the communication was made, and (b) a notice, circular, advertisement, letter, or communication in respect of a security shall not be deemed to be a prospectus if it states from whom a written prospectus meeting the requirements of section 10 may be obtained and, in addition, does no more than identify the security, state the price thereof, state by whom orders will be executed, and contain such other information as the Commission, by rules or regulations deemed necessary or appropriate in the public interest and for the protection of investors, and subject to such terms and conditions as may be prescribed therein, may permit.

(11) The term "underwriter" means any person who has purchased from an issuer with a view to, or offers or sells for an issuer in connection with, the distribution of any security, or participates or has a direct or indirect participation in any such undertaking, or participates or has a participation in the direct or indirect underwriting of any such undertaking; but such term shall not include a person whose interest is limited to a commission from an underwriter or dealer not in excess of the usual and customary distributors' or sellers' commission. As used in this paragraph the term "issuer" shall include, in addition to an issuer, any person directly or indirectly controlling or controlled by the issuer, or any person under direct or indirect common control with the issuer.

(12) The term "dealer" means any person who engages either for all or part of his time, directly or indirectly, as agent, broker, or principal, in the business of offering, buying, selling, or otherwise dealing or trading in securities issued by another person.

(13) The term "insurance company" means a company which is organized as an insurance company, whose primary and predominant business activity is the writing of insurance or the reinsuring of risks underwritten by insurance companies, and which is subject to supervision by the insurance commissioner, or a similar official or agency, of a State or territory or the District of Columbia; or any receiver or similar official or any liquidating agent for such company, in his capacity as such.

(14) The term "separate account" means an account established and maintained by an insurance company pursuant to the laws of any State or territory of the United States, the District of Columbia, or of Canada or any province thereof, under which income, gains and losses, whether or not realized, from assets allocated to such account, are, in accordance with the applicable contract, credited to or charged against such account without regard to other income, gains, or losses of the insurance company.

(15) The term "accredited investor" shall mean—

(i) a bank as defined in section 3(a)(2) whether acting in its individual or fiduciary capacity; an insurance company as defined in paragraph (13) of this subsection; an investment company registered under the Investment Company Act of 1940 or a business development company as defined in section 2(a)(48) of that Act; a Small Business Investment Company licensed by the Small Business Administration; or an employee benefit plan, including an individual retirement account, which is subject to the provisions of the Employee Retirement Income Security Act of 1974,[2] if the investment decision is made by a plan fiduciary, as defined in section 3(21) of such Act, which is either a bank, insurance company, or registered investment adviser; or

(ii) any person who, on the basis of such factors as financial sophistication, net worth, knowledge, and experience in financial matters, or amount of assets under management qualifies as an accredited investor under rules and regulations which the Commission shall prescribe.

(16) The terms "security future", "narrow-based security index", and "security futures product" have the same meanings as provided in section 3(a)(55) of the Securities Exchange Act of 1934.

(17) The terms "swap" and "security-based swap" have the same meanings as in section 1a of the Commodity Exchange Act (7 U.S.C. 1a).

(18) The terms "purchase" or "sale" of a security-based swap shall be deemed to mean the execution, termination (prior to its scheduled maturity date), assignment, exchange, or similar transfer or conveyance of, or extinguishing of rights or obligations under, a security-based swap, as the context may require.

(19) The term "emerging growth company" means an issuer that had total annual gross revenues of less than $1,000,000,000 (as such amount is indexed for inflation every 5 years by the Commission to reflect the change in the Consumer Price Index for All Urban Consumers published by the Bureau of Labor Statistics, setting the threshold to the nearest 1,000,000) during its most recently completed fiscal year. An issuer that is an emerging growth company as of the first day of that fiscal year shall continue to be deemed an emerging growth company until the earliest of—

(A) the last day of the fiscal year of the issuer during which it had total annual gross revenues of $1,000,000,000 (as such amount is indexed for inflation every 5 years by the Commission to reflect the change in the Consumer Price Index for All Urban Consumers published by the Bureau of Labor Statistics, setting the threshold to the nearest 1,000,000) or more;

(B) the last day of the fiscal year of the issuer following the fifth anniversary of the date of the first sale of

---

[2] 29 U.S.C. 1001 et seq. [Printed in appendix to this volume.]

common equity securities of the issuer pursuant to an effective registration statement under this title;

(C) the date on which such issuer has, during the previous 3-year period, issued more than $1,000,000,000 in non-convertible debt; or

(D) the date on which such issuer is deemed to be a "large accelerated filer", as defined in section 240.12b–2 of title 17, Code of Federal Regulations, or any successor thereto.

(b) CONSIDERATION OF PROMOTION OF EFFICIENCY, COMPETITION, AND CAPITAL FORMATION.—Whenever pursuant to this title the Commission is engaged in rulemaking and is required to consider or determine whether an action is necessary or appropriate in the public interest, the Commission shall also consider, in addition to the protection of investors, whether the action will promote efficiency, competition, and capital formation.

SEC. 2A. [77b–1] SWAP AGREEMENTS.

(a) Reserved.

(b) SECURITY-BASED SWAP AGREEMENTS.—

(1) The definition of "security" in section 2(a)(1) of this title does not include any security-based swap agreement (as defined in section 3(a)(78) of the Securities Exchange Act of 1934).

(2) The Commission is prohibited from registering, or requiring, recommending, or suggesting, the registration under this title of any security-based swap agreement (as defined in section 3(a)(78) of the Securities Exchange Act of 1934). If the Commission becomes aware that a registrant has filed a registration statement with respect to such a swap agreement, the Commission shall promptly so notify the registrant. Any such registration statement with respect to such a swap agreement shall be void and of no force or effect.

(3) The Commission is prohibited from—

(A) promulgating, interpreting, or enforcing rules; or

(B) issuing orders of general applicability;

under this title in a manner that imposes or specifies reporting or recordkeeping requirements, procedures, or standards as prophylactic measures against fraud, manipulation, or insider trading with respect to any security-based swap agreement (as defined in section 3(a)(78) of the Securities Exchange Act of 1934).

(4) References in this title to the "purchase" or "sale" of a security-based swap agreement shall be deemed to mean the execution, termination (prior to its scheduled maturity date), assignment, exchange, or similar transfer or conveyance of, or extinguishing of rights or obligations under, a security-based swap agreement (as defined in section 3(a)(78) of the Securities Exchange Act of 1934), as the context may require.

EXEMPTED SECURITIES [3]

SEC. 3. [77c] (a) Except as hereinafter expressly provided, the provisions of this title shall not apply to any of the following classes of securities:
  (1) Reserved.
  (2) Any security issued or guaranteed by the United States or any Territory thereof, or by the District of Columbia, or by any State of the United States, or by any political subdivision of a State or Territory, or by any public instrumentality of one or more States or Territories, or by any person controlled or supervised by and acting as an instrumentality of the Government of the United States pursuant to authority granted by the Congress of the United States; or any certificate of deposit for any of the foregoing; or any security issued or guaranteed by any bank; or any security issued by or representing an interest in or a direct obligation of a Federal Reserve bank; or any interest or participation in any common trust fund or similar fund that is excluded from the definition of the term "investment company" under section 3(c)(3) of the Investment Company Act of 1940; or any security which is an industrial development bond (as defined in section 103(c)(2) of the Internal Revenue Code of 1954) [4] the interest on which is excludable from gross income under section 103(a)(1) of such Code if, by reason of the application of paragraph (4) or (6) of section 103(c) of such Code (determined as if paragraphs (4)(A), (5), and (7) [5] were not included in such section 103(c)), paragraph (1) of such section 103(c) does not apply to such security; or any interest or participation in a single trust fund, or in a collective trust fund maintained by a bank, or any security arising out of a contract issued by an insurance company, which interest, participation, or security is issued in connection with (A) a stock bonus, pension, or profit-sharing plan which meets the requirements for qualification under section 401 of the Internal Revenue Code of 1954, [6] (B) an annuity plan which meets the requirements for the deduction of the employer's contributions under section 404(a)(2) of such Code, [7] (C) a governmental plan as defined in section 414(d) of such Code [8] which has been established by an employer for the exclusive benefit of its employees or their beneficiaries for the purpose of distributing to such employees or their beneficiaries the corpus and income of the funds accumulated under such plan, if under such plan it is impossible, prior to the satisfaction of all liabilities with respect to such employees and their beneficiaries, for any part of the corpus or income to be used for,

---

[3] Additional exemptions contained at: 7 U.S.C. 1932(d)(6); 12 U.S.C. 1455, 1717, 1719, 1723c; 15 U.S.C. 77c, note; 20 U.S.C. 1087–2, 1087hh; 22 U.S.C. 283(h), 285h, 286k–1, 290i–9; 43 U.S.C. 1625; and 45 U.S.C. 720. [Printed in appendix to this volume except for 7 U.S.C. 1932(d)(6) and 15 U.S.C. 77c.]
[4] Section 103(c) of the Internal Revenue Code of 1954 redesignated as section 103(b) by section 1901(a)(17) of Pub. L. 94–455 (26 U.S.C. 103(b)). [Printed in appendix to this volume.]
[5] Paragraph (7) redesignated as paragraph (13) (26 U.S.C. 103(b)(13)). [Printed in appendix to this volume.]
[6] 26 U.S.C. 401. [Printed in appendix to this volume.]
[7] 26 U.S.C. 404(a)(2). [Printed in appendix to this volume.]
[8] 26 U.S.C. 414(d). [Printed in appendix to this volume.]

or diverted to, purposes other than the exclusive benefit of such employees or their beneficiaries, or (D) a church plan, company, or account that is excluded from the definition of an investment company under section 3(c)(14) of the Investment Company Act of 1940, other than any plan described in subparagraph (A), (B), (C), or (D) of this paragraph (i) the contributions under which are held in a single trust fund or in a separate account maintained by an insurance company for a single employer and under which an amount in excess of the employer's contribution is allocated to the purchase of securities (other than interests or participations in the trust or separate account itself) issued by the employer or any company directly or indirectly controlling, controlled by, or under common control with the employer, (ii) which covers employees some or all of whom are employees within the meaning of section 401(c)(1) of such Code (other than a person participating in a church plan who is described in section 414(e)(3)(B) of the Internal Revenue Code of 1986), or (iii) which is a plan funded by an annuity contract described in section 403(b)[9] of such Code (other than a retirement income account described in section 403(b)(9) of the Internal Revenue Code of 1986, to the extent that the interest or participation in such single trust fund or collective trust fund is issued to a church, a convention or association of churches, or an organization described in section 414(e)(3)(A) of such Code establishing or maintaining the retirement income account or to a trust established by any such entity in connection with the retirement income account). The Commission, by rules and regulations or order, shall exempt from the provisions of section 5 of this title any interest or participation issued in connection with a stock bonus, pension, profit-sharing, or annuity plan which covers employees some or all of whom are employees within the meaning of section 401(c)(1) of the Internal Revenue Code of 1954, if and to the extent that the Commission determines this to be necessary or appropriate in the public interest and consistent with the protection of investors and the purposes fairly intended by the policy and provisions of this title. For purposes of this paragraph, a security issued or guaranteed by a bank shall not include any interest or participation in any collective trust fund maintained by a bank; and the term "bank" means any national bank, or any banking institution organized under the laws of any State, territory, or the District of Columbia, the business of which is substantially confined to banking and is supervised by the State or territorial banking commission or similar official; except that in the case of a common trust fund or similar fund, or a collective trust fund, the term "bank" has the same meaning as in the Investment Company Act of 1940;

(3) Any note, draft, bill of exchange, or banker's acceptance which arises out of a current transaction or the proceeds of which have been or are to be used for current transactions, and which has a maturity at the time of issuance of not exceeding

---

[9] 26 U.S.C. 403(b). [Printed in appendix to this volume.]

nine months, exclusive of days of grace, or any renewal thereof the maturity of which is likewise limited;

(4) Any security issued by a person organized and operated exclusively for religious, educational, benevolent, fraternal, charitable, or reformatory purposes and not for pecuniary profit, and no part of the net earnings of which inures to the benefit of any person, private stockholder, or individual, or any security of a fund that is excluded from the definition of an investment company under section 3(c)(10)(B) of the Investment Company Act of 1940;

(5) Any security issued (A) by a savings and loan association, building and loan association, cooperative bank, homestead association, or similar institution, which is supervised and examined by State or Federal authority having supervision over any such institution; or (B) by (i) a farmer's cooperative organization exempt from tax under section 521 of the Internal Revenue Code of 1954, [10] (ii) a corporation described in section 501(c)(16) of such Code [11] and exempt from tax under section 501(a) of such Code, or (iii) a corporation described in section 501(c)(2) of such Code which is exempt from tax under section 501(a) of such Code and is organized for the exclusive purpose of holding title to property, collecting income therefrom, and turning over the entire amount thereof, less expenses, to an organization or corporation described in clause (i) or (ii);

(6) Any interest in a railroad equipment trust. For purposes of this paragraph "interest in a railroad equipment trust" means any interest in an equipment trust, lease, conditional sales contract, or other similar arrangement entered into, issued, assumed, guaranteed by, or for the benefit of, a common carrier to finance the acquisition of rolling stock, including motive power;

(7) Certificates issued by a receiver or by a trustee in bankruptcy, with the approval of the court;

(8) Any insurance or endowment policy or annuity contract or optional annuity contract, issued by a corporation subject to the supervision of the insurance commissioner, bank commissioner, or any agency or officer performing like functions, of any State or Territory of the United States or the District of Columbia; [12]

(9) Except with respect to a security exchanged in a case under title 11, any security exchanged by the issuer with its existing security holders exclusively where no commission or other remuneration is paid or given directly or indirectly for soliciting such exchange;

(10) Except with respect to a security exchanged in a case under title 11, any security which is issued in exchange for one or more bona fide outstanding securities, claims or property interests, or partly in such exchange and partly for cash, where the terms and conditions of such issuance and exchange are approved, after a hearing upon the fairness of such terms and conditions at which all persons to whom it is proposed to issue

---

[10] 26 U.S.C. 521. [Printed in appendix to this volume.]
[11] 26 U.S.C. 501(c)(16). [Printed in appendix to this volume.]
[12] But see section 24(d) of the Investment Company Act of 1940, infra.

securities in such exchange shall have the right to appear, by any court, or by any official or agency of the United States, or by any State or Territorial banking or insurance commission or other governmental authority expressly authorized by law to grant such approval;

(11) Any security which is a part of an issue offered and sold only to persons resident within a single State or Territory, where the issuer of such security is a person resident and doing business within or, if a corporation, incorporated by and doing business within, such State or Territory.

(12) Any equity security issued in connection with the acquisition by a holding company of a bank under section 3(a) of the Bank Holding Company Act of 1956 or a savings association under section 10(e) of the Home Owners' Loan Act, if—

(A) the acquisition occurs solely as part of a reorganization in which security holders exchange their shares of a bank or savings association for shares of a newly formed holding company with no significant assets other than securities of the bank or savings association and the existing subsidiaries of the bank or savings association;

(B) the security holders receive, after that reorganization, substantially the same proportional share interests in the holding company as they held in the bank or savings association, except for nominal changes in shareholders' interests resulting from lawful elimination of fractional interests and the exercise of dissenting shareholders' rights under State or Federal law;

(C) the rights and interests of security holders in the holding company are substantially the same as those in the bank or savings association prior to the transaction, other than as may be required by law; and

(D) the holding company has substantially the same assets and liabilities, on a consolidated basis, as the bank or savings association had prior to the transaction.

For purposes of this paragraph, the term "savings association" means a savings association (as defined in section 3(b) of the Federal Deposit Insurance Act) the deposits of which are insured by the Federal Deposit Insurance Corporation.

(13) Any security issued by or any interest or participation in any church plan, company or account that is excluded from the definition of an investment company under section 3(c)(14) of the Investment Company Act of 1940.

(14) Any security futures product that is—

(A) cleared by a clearing agency registered under section 17A of the Securities Exchange Act of 1934 or exempt from registration under subsection (b)(7) of such section 17A; and

(B) traded on a national securities exchange or a national securities association registered pursuant to section 15A(a) of the Securities Exchange Act of 1934.

(b) ADDITIONAL EXEMPTIONS.—

(1) SMALL ISSUES EXEMPTIVE AUTHORITY.—The Commission may from time to time by its rules and regulations, and subject to such terms and conditions as may be prescribed therein, add

any class of securities to the securities exempted as provided in this section, if it finds that the enforcement of this title with respect to such securities is not necessary in the public interest and for the protection of investors by reason of the small amount involved or the limited character of the public offering; but no issue of securities shall be exempted under this subsection where the aggregate amount at which such issue is offered to the public exceeds $5,000,000.

(2) ADDITIONAL ISSUES.—The Commission shall by rule or regulation add a class of securities to the securities exempted pursuant to this section in accordance with the following terms and conditions:

(A) The aggregate offering amount of all securities offered and sold within the prior 12-month period in reliance on the exemption added in accordance with this paragraph shall not exceed $50,000,000.

(B) The securities may be offered and sold publicly.

(C) The securities shall not be restricted securities within the meaning of the Federal securities laws and the regulations promulgated thereunder.

(D) The civil liability provision in section 12(a)(2) shall apply to any person offering or selling such securities.

(E) The issuer may solicit interest in the offering prior to filing any offering statement, on such terms and conditions as the Commission may prescribe in the public interest or for the protection of investors.

(F) The Commission shall require the issuer to file audited financial statements with the Commission annually.

(G) Such other terms, conditions, or requirements as the Commission may determine necessary in the public interest and for the protection of investors, which may include—

(i) a requirement that the issuer prepare and electronically file with the Commission and distribute to prospective investors an offering statement, and any related documents, in such form and with such content as prescribed by the Commission, including audited financial statements, a description of the issuer's business operations, its financial condition, its corporate governance principles, its use of investor funds, and other appropriate matters; and

(ii) disqualification provisions under which the exemption shall not be available to the issuer or its predecessors, affiliates, officers, directors, underwriters, or other related persons, which shall be substantially similar to the disqualification provisions contained in the regulations adopted in accordance with section 926 of the Dodd-Frank Wall Street Reform and Consumer Protection Act (15 U.S.C. 77d note).

(3) LIMITATION.—Only the following types of securities may be exempted under a rule or regulation adopted pursuant to paragraph (2): equity securities, debt securities, and debt secu-

rities convertible or exchangeable to equity interests, including any guarantees of such securities.

(4) PERIODIC DISCLOSURES.—Upon such terms and conditions as the Commission determines necessary in the public interest and for the protection of investors, the Commission by rule or regulation may require an issuer of a class of securities exempted under paragraph (2) to make available to investors and file with the Commission periodic disclosures regarding the issuer, its business operations, its financial condition, its corporate governance principles, its use of investor funds, and other appropriate matters, and also may provide for the suspension and termination of such a requirement with respect to that issuer.

(5) ADJUSTMENT.—Not later than 2 years after the date of enactment of the Small Company Capital Formation Act of 2011 [13] and every 2 years thereafter, the Commission shall review the offering amount limitation described in paragraph (2)(A) and shall increase such amount as the Commission determines appropriate. If the Commission determines not to increase such amount, it shall report to the Committee on Financial Services of the House of Representatives and the Committee on Banking, Housing, and Urban Affairs of the Senate on its reasons for not increasing the amount.

(c) The Commission may from time to time by its rules and regulations and subject to such terms and conditions as may be prescribed therein, add to the securities exempted as provided in this section any class of securities issued by a small business investment company under the Small Business Investment Act of 1958 [14] if it finds, having regard to the purposes of that Act, that the enforcement of this Act with respect to such securities is not necessary in the public interest and for the protection of investors.

EXEMPTED TRANSACTIONS [15]

SEC. 4. 【77d】 (a) The provisions of section 5 shall not apply to—

(1) transactions by any person other than an issuer, underwriter, or dealer.

(2) transactions by an issuer not involving any public offering.

(3) transactions by a dealer (including an underwriter no longer acting as an underwriter in respect of the security involved in such transaction), except—

(A) transactions taking place prior to the expiration of forty days after the first date upon which the security was bona fide offered to the public by the issuer or by or through an underwriter,

(B) transactions in a security as to which a registration statement has been filed taking place prior to the expiration of forty days after the effective date of such reg-

---

[13] The reference to the Small Company Capital Formation Act of 2011 in this paragraph probably should be a reference to the Jumpstart Our Business Startups Act.
[14] 15 U.S.C. 661 et seq.
[15] See additional exemption contained at 11 U.S.C. 1145.

istration statement or prior to the expiration of forty days after the first date upon which the security was bona fide offered to the public by the issuer or by or through an underwriter after such effective date, whichever is later (excluding in the computation of such forty days any time during which a stop order issued under section 8 is in effect as to the security), or such shorter period as the Commission may specify by rules and regulations or order, and

(C) transactions as to securities constituting the whole or a part of an unsold allotment to or subscription by such dealer as a participant in the distribution of such securities by the issuer or by or through an underwriter.

With respect to transactions referred to in clause (B), if securities of the issuer have not previously been sold pursuant to an earlier effective registration statement the applicable period, instead of forty days, shall be ninety days, or such shorter period as the Commission may specify by rules and regulations or order.

(4) brokers' transactions executed upon customers' orders on any exchange or in the over-the-counter market but not the solicitation of such orders.

(5) transactions involving offers or sales by an issuer solely to one or more accredited investors, if the aggregate offering price of an issue of securities offered in reliance on this paragraph does not exceed the amount allowed under section 3(b)(1) of this title, if there is no advertising or public solicitation in connection with the transaction by the issuer or anyone acting on the issuer's behalf, and if the issuer files such notice with the Commission as the Commission shall prescribe.

(6) transactions involving the offer or sale of securities by an issuer (including all entities controlled by or under common control with the issuer), provided that—

(A) the aggregate amount sold to all investors by the issuer, including any amount sold in reliance on the exemption provided under this paragraph during the 12-month period preceding the date of such transaction, is not more than $1,000,000;

(B) the aggregate amount sold to any investor by an issuer, including any amount sold in reliance on the exemption provided under this paragraph during the 12-month period preceding the date of such transaction, does not exceed—

(i) the greater of $2,000 or 5 percent of the annual income or net worth of such investor, as applicable, if either the annual income or the net worth of the investor is less than $100,000; and

(ii) 10 percent of the annual income or net worth of such investor, as applicable, not to exceed a maximum aggregate amount sold of $100,000, if either the annual income or net worth of the investor is equal to or more than $100,000;

(C) the transaction is conducted through a broker or funding portal that complies with the requirements of section 4A(a); and

(D) the issuer complies with the requirements of section 4A(b).

(7) transactions meeting the requirements of subsection (d).

(b) Offers and sales exempt under section 230.506 of title 17, Code of Federal Regulations (as revised pursuant to section 201 of the Jumpstart Our Business Startups Act) shall not be deemed public offerings under the Federal securities laws as a result of general advertising or general solicitation.

(c)(1) With respect to securities offered and sold in compliance with Rule 506 of Regulation D under this Act, no person who meets the conditions set forth in paragraph (2) shall be subject to registration as a broker or dealer pursuant to section 15(a)(1) of this title [17], solely because—

(A) that person maintains a platform or mechanism that permits the offer, sale, purchase, or negotiation of or with respect to securities, or permits general solicitations, general advertisements, or similar or related activities by issuers of such securities, whether online, in person, or through any other means;

(B) that person or any person associated with that person co-invests in such securities; or

(C) that person or any person associated with that person provides ancillary services with respect to such securities.

(2) The exemption provided in paragraph (1) shall apply to any person described in such paragraph if—

(A) such person and each person associated with that person receives no compensation in connection with the purchase or sale of such security;

(B) such person and each person associated with that person does not have possession of customer funds or securities in connection with the purchase or sale of such security; and

(C) such person is not subject to a statutory disqualification as defined in section 3(a)(39) of this title and does not have any person associated with that person subject to such a statutory disqualification.

(3) For the purposes of this subsection, the term "ancillary services" means—

(A) the provision of due diligence services, in connection with the offer, sale, purchase, or negotiation of such security, so long as such services do not include, for separate compensation, investment advice or recommendations to issuers or investors; and

(B) the provision of standardized documents to the issuers and investors, so long as such person or entity does not negotiate the terms of the issuance for and on behalf of third parties and issuers are not required to use the standardized documents as a condition of using the service.

---

[17] The reference to "section 15(a)(1) of this title" in subsection (b)(1) probably should be a reference to "section 15(a)(1) of the Securities Exchange Act of 1934".

(d) CERTAIN ACCREDITED INVESTOR TRANSACTIONS.—The transactions referred to in subsection (a)(7) are transactions meeting the following requirements:

(1) ACCREDITED INVESTOR REQUIREMENT.—Each purchaser is an accredited investor, as that term is defined in section 230.501(a) of title 17, Code of Federal Regulations (or any successor regulation).

(2) PROHIBITION ON GENERAL SOLICITATION OR ADVERTISING.—Neither the seller, nor any person acting on the seller's behalf, offers or sells securities by any form of general solicitation or general advertising.

(3) INFORMATION REQUIREMENT.—In the case of a transaction involving the securities of an issuer that is neither subject to section 13 or 15(d) of the Securities Exchange Act of 1934 (15 U.S.C. 78m; 78o(d)), nor exempt from reporting pursuant to section 240.12g3–2(b) of title 17, Code of Federal Regulations, nor a foreign government (as defined in section 230.405 of title 17, Code of Federal Regulations) eligible to register securities under Schedule B, the seller and a prospective purchaser designated by the seller obtain from the issuer, upon request of the seller, and the seller in all cases makes available to a prospective purchaser, the following information (which shall be reasonably current in relation to the date of resale under this section):

(A) The exact name of the issuer and the issuer's predecessor (if any).

(B) The address of the issuer's principal executive offices.

(C) The exact title and class of the security.

(D) The par or stated value of the security.

(E) The number of shares or total amount of the securities outstanding as of the end of the issuer's most recent fiscal year.

(F) The name and address of the transfer agent, corporate secretary, or other person responsible for transferring shares and stock certificates.

(G) A statement of the nature of the business of the issuer and the products and services it offers, which shall be presumed reasonably current if the statement is as of 12 months before the transaction date.

(H) The names of the officers and directors of the issuer.

(I) The names of any persons registered as a broker, dealer, or agent that shall be paid or given, directly or indirectly, any commission or remuneration for such person's participation in the offer or sale of the securities.

(J) The issuer's most recent balance sheet and profit and loss statement and similar financial statements, which shall—

(i) be for such part of the 2 preceding fiscal years as the issuer has been in operation;

(ii) be prepared in accordance with generally accepted accounting principles or, in the case of a foreign private issuer, be prepared in accordance with gen-

erally accepted accounting principles or the International Financial Reporting Standards issued by the International Accounting Standards Board;
    (iii) be presumed reasonably current if—
        (I) with respect to the balance sheet, the balance sheet is as of a date less than 16 months before the transaction date; and
        (II) with respect to the profit and loss statement, such statement is for the 12 months preceding the date of the issuer's balance sheet; and
    (iv) if the balance sheet is not as of a date less than 6 months before the transaction date, be accompanied by additional statements of profit and loss for the period from the date of such balance sheet to a date less than 6 months before the transaction date.
    (K) To the extent that the seller is a control person with respect to the issuer, a brief statement regarding the nature of the affiliation, and a statement certified by such seller that they have no reasonable grounds to believe that the issuer is in violation of the securities laws or regulations.
  (4) ISSUERS DISQUALIFIED.—The transaction is not for the sale of a security where the seller is an issuer or a subsidiary, either directly or indirectly, of the issuer.
  (5) BAD ACTOR PROHIBITION.—Neither the seller, nor any person that has been or will be paid (directly or indirectly) remuneration or a commission for their participation in the offer or sale of the securities, including solicitation of purchasers for the seller is subject to an event that would disqualify an issuer or other covered person under Rule 506(d)(1) of Regulation D (17 CFR 230.506(d)(1)) or is subject to a statutory disqualification described under section 3(a)(39) of the Securities Exchange Act of 1934.
  (6) BUSINESS REQUIREMENT.—The issuer is engaged in business, is not in the organizational stage or in bankruptcy or receivership, and is not a blank check, blind pool, or shell company that has no specific business plan or purpose or has indicated that the issuer's primary business plan is to engage in a merger or combination of the business with, or an acquisition of, an unidentified person.
  (7) UNDERWRITER PROHIBITION.—The transaction is not with respect to a security that constitutes the whole or part of an unsold allotment to, or a subscription or participation by, a broker or dealer as an underwriter of the security or a redistribution.
  (8) OUTSTANDING CLASS REQUIREMENT.—The transaction is with respect to a security of a class that has been authorized and outstanding for at least 90 days prior to the date of the transaction.
(e) ADDITIONAL REQUIREMENTS.—
  (1) IN GENERAL.—With respect to an exempted transaction described under subsection (a)(7):

(A) Securities acquired in such transaction shall be deemed to have been acquired in a transaction not involving any public offering.

(B) Such transaction shall be deemed not to be a distribution for purposes of section 2(a)(11).

(C) Securities involved in such transaction shall be deemed to be restricted securities within the meaning of Rule 144 (17 CFR 230.144).

(2) RULE OF CONSTRUCTION.—The exemption provided by subsection (a)(7) shall not be the exclusive means for establishing an exemption from the registration requirements of section 5.

SEC. 4A. [77d-1] **REQUIREMENTS WITH RESPECT TO CERTAIN SMALL TRANSACTIONS.**[18]

(a) REQUIREMENTS ON INTERMEDIARIES.—A person acting as an intermediary in a transaction involving the offer or sale of securities for the account of others pursuant to section 4(6) shall—

(1) register with the Commission as—

(A) a broker; or

(B) a funding portal (as defined in section 3(a)(80) of the Securities Exchange Act of 1934);

(2) register with any applicable self-regulatory organization (as defined in section 3(a)(26) of the Securities Exchange Act of 1934);

(3) provide such disclosures, including disclosures related to risks and other investor education materials, as the Commission shall, by rule, determine appropriate;

(4) ensure that each investor—

(A) reviews investor-education information, in accordance with standards established by the Commission, by rule;

(B) positively affirms that the investor understands that the investor is risking the loss of the entire investment, and that the investor could bear such a loss; and

(C) answers questions demonstrating—

(i) an understanding of the level of risk generally applicable to investments in startups, emerging businesses, and small issuers;

(ii) an understanding of the risk of illiquidity; and

(iii) an understanding of such other matters as the Commission determines appropriate, by rule;

(5) take such measures to reduce the risk of fraud with respect to such transactions, as established by the Commission, by rule, including obtaining a background and securities enforcement regulatory history check on each officer, director, and person holding more than 20 percent of the outstanding equity of every issuer whose securities are offered by such person;

(6) not later than 21 days prior to the first day on which securities are sold to any investor (or such other period as the Commission may establish), make available to the Commission

---

[18] All references to section 4(6) throughout this section probably should be a reference to section 4(a)(6).

and to potential investors any information provided by the issuer pursuant to subsection (b);

(7) ensure that all offering proceeds are only provided to the issuer when the aggregate capital raised from all investors is equal to or greater than a target offering amount, and allow all investors to cancel their commitments to invest, as the Commission shall, by rule, determine appropriate;

(8) make such efforts as the Commission determines appropriate, by rule, to ensure that no investor in a 12-month period has purchased securities offered pursuant to section 4(6) that, in the aggregate, from all issuers, exceed the investment limits set forth in section 4(6)(B);

(9) take such steps to protect the privacy of information collected from investors as the Commission shall, by rule, determine appropriate;

(10) not compensate promoters, finders, or lead generators for providing the broker or funding portal with the personal identifying information of any potential investor;

(11) prohibit its directors, officers, or partners (or any person occupying a similar status or performing a similar function) from having any financial interest in an issuer using its services; and

(12) meet such other requirements as the Commission may, by rule, prescribe, for the protection of investors and in the public interest.

(b) REQUIREMENTS FOR ISSUERS.—For purposes of section 4(6), an issuer who offers or sells securities shall—

(1) file with the Commission and provide to investors and the relevant broker or funding portal, and make available to potential investors—

(A) the name, legal status, physical address, and website address of the issuer;

(B) the names of the directors and officers (and any persons occupying a similar status or performing a similar function), and each person holding more than 20 percent of the shares of the issuer;

(C) a description of the business of the issuer and the anticipated business plan of the issuer;

(D) a description of the financial condition of the issuer, including, for offerings that, together with all other offerings of the issuer under section 4(6) within the preceding 12-month period, have, in the aggregate, target offering amounts of—

(i) $100,000 or less—

(I) the income tax returns filed by the issuer for the most recently completed year (if any); and

(II) financial statements of the issuer, which shall be certified by the principal executive officer of the issuer to be true and complete in all material respects;

(ii) more than $100,000, but not more than $500,000, financial statements reviewed by a public accountant who is independent of the issuer, using professional standards and procedures for such review or standards and procedures established by the Commission, by rule, for such purpose; and

(iii) more than $500,000 (or such other amount as the Commission may establish, by rule), audited financial statements;

(E) a description of the stated purpose and intended use of the proceeds of the offering sought by the issuer with respect to the target offering amount;

(F) the target offering amount, the deadline to reach the target offering amount, and regular updates regarding the progress of the issuer in meeting the target offering amount;

(G) the price to the public of the securities or the method for determining the price, provided that, prior to sale, each investor shall be provided in writing the final price and all required disclosures, with a reasonable opportunity to rescind the commitment to purchase the securities;

(H) a description of the ownership and capital structure of the issuer, including—

(i) terms of the securities of the issuer being offered and each other class of security of the issuer, including how such terms may be modified, and a summary of the differences between such securities, including how the rights of the securities being offered may be materially limited, diluted, or qualified by the rights of any other class of security of the issuer;

(ii) a description of how the exercise of the rights held by the principal shareholders of the issuer could negatively impact the purchasers of the securities being offered;

(iii) the name and ownership level of each existing shareholder who owns more than 20 percent of any class of the securities of the issuer;

(iv) how the securities being offered are being valued, and examples of methods for how such securities may be valued by the issuer in the future, including during subsequent corporate actions; and

(v) the risks to purchasers of the securities relating to minority ownership in the issuer, the risks associated with corporate actions, including additional issuances of shares, a sale of the issuer or of assets of the issuer, or transactions with related parties; and

(I) such other information as the Commission may, by rule, prescribe, for the protection of investors and in the public interest;

(2) not advertise the terms of the offering, except for notices which direct investors to the funding portal or broker;

(3) not compensate or commit to compensate, directly or indirectly, any person to promote its offerings through communication channels provided by a broker or funding portal, without taking such steps as the Commission shall, by rule, require to ensure that such person clearly discloses the receipt, past or

prospective, of such compensation, upon each instance of such promotional communication;

(4) not less than annually, file with the Commission and provide to investors reports of the results of operations and financial statements of the issuer, as the Commission shall, by rule, determine appropriate, subject to such exceptions and termination dates as the Commission may establish, by rule; and

(5) comply with such other requirements as the Commission may, by rule, prescribe, for the protection of investors and in the public interest.

(c) LIABILITY FOR MATERIAL MISSTATEMENTS AND OMISSIONS.—
  (1) ACTIONS AUTHORIZED.—
    (A) IN GENERAL.—Subject to paragraph (2), a person who purchases a security in a transaction exempted by the provisions of section 4(6) may bring an action against an issuer described in paragraph (2), either at law or in equity in any court of competent jurisdiction, to recover the consideration paid for such security with interest thereon, less the amount of any income received thereon, upon the tender of such security, or for damages if such person no longer owns the security.
    (B) LIABILITY.—An action brought under this paragraph shall be subject to the provisions of section 12(b) and section 13, as if the liability were created under section 12(a)(2).
  (2) APPLICABILITY.—An issuer shall be liable in an action under paragraph (1), if the issuer—
    (A) by the use of any means or instruments of transportation or communication in interstate commerce or of the mails, by any means of any written or oral communication, in the offering or sale of a security in a transaction exempted by the provisions of section 4(6), makes an untrue statement of a material fact or omits to state a material fact required to be stated or necessary in order to make the statements, in the light of the circumstances under which they were made, not misleading, provided that the purchaser did not know of such untruth or omission; and
    (B) does not sustain the burden of proof that such issuer did not know, and in the exercise of reasonable care could not have known, of such untruth or omission.
  (3) DEFINITION.—As used in this subsection, the term "issuer" includes any person who is a director or partner of the issuer, and the principal executive officer or officers, principal financial officer, and controller or principal accounting officer of the issuer (and any person occupying a similar status or performing a similar function) that offers or sells a security in a transaction exempted by the provisions of section 4(6), and any person who offers or sells the security in such offering.

(d) INFORMATION AVAILABLE TO STATES.—The Commission shall make, or shall cause to be made by the relevant broker or funding portal, the information described in subsection (b) and such other information as the Commission, by rule, determines appropriate, available to the securities commission (or any agency or office performing like functions) of each State and territory of the United States and the District of Columbia.

(e) RESTRICTIONS ON SALES.—Securities issued pursuant to a transaction described in section 4(6)—

(1) may not be transferred by the purchaser of such securities during the 1-year period beginning on the date of purchase, unless such securities are transferred—

(A) to the issuer of the securities;
(B) to an accredited investor;
(C) as part of an offering registered with the Commission; or
(D) to a member of the family of the purchaser or the equivalent, or in connection with the death or divorce of the purchaser or other similar circumstance, in the discretion of the Commission; and

(2) shall be subject to such other limitations as the Commission shall, by rule, establish.

(f) APPLICABILITY.—Section 4(6) shall not apply to transactions involving the offer or sale of securities by any issuer that—

(1) is not organized under and subject to the laws of a State or territory of the United States or the District of Columbia;

(2) is subject to the requirement to file reports pursuant to section 13 or section 15(d) of the Securities Exchange Act of 1934;

(3) is an investment company, as defined in section 3 of the Investment Company Act of 1940, or is excluded from the definition of investment company by section 3(b) or section 3(c) of that Act; or

(4) the Commission, by rule or regulation, determines appropriate.

(g) RULE OF CONSTRUCTION.—Nothing in this section or section 4(6) shall be construed as preventing an issuer from raising capital through methods not described under section 4(6).

(h) CERTAIN CALCULATIONS.—

(1) DOLLAR AMOUNTS.—Dollar amounts in section 4(6) and subsection (b) of this section shall be adjusted by the Commission not less frequently than once every 5 years, by notice published in the Federal Register to reflect any change in the Consumer Price Index for All Urban Consumers published by the Bureau of Labor Statistics.

(2) INCOME AND NET WORTH.—The income and net worth of a natural person under section 4(6)(B) shall be calculated in accordance with any rules of the Commission under this title regarding the calculation of the income and net worth, respectively, of an accredited investor.

PROHIBITIONS RELATING TO INTERSTATE COMMERCE AND THE MAILS

SEC. 5. [77e] (a) Unless a registration statement is in effect as to a security, it shall be unlawful for any person, directly or indirectly—

(1) to make use of any means or instruments of transportation or communication in interstate commerce or of the mails

to sell such security through the use or medium of any prospectus or otherwise; or

(2) to carry or cause to be carried through the mails or in interstate commerce, by any means or instruments of transportation, any such security for the purpose of sale or for delivery after sale.

(b) It shall be unlawful for any person, directly or indirectly—

(1) to make use of any means or instruments of transportation or communication in interstate commerce or of the mails to carry or transmit any prospectus relating to any security with respect to which a registration statement has been filed under this title, unless such prospectus meets the requirements of section 10; or

(2) to carry or cause to be carried through the mails or in interstate commerce any such security for the purpose of sale or for delivery after sale, unless accompanied or preceded by a prospectus that meets the requirements of subsection (a) of section 10.

(c) It shall be unlawful for any person, directly or indirectly, to make use of any means or instruments of transportation or communication in interstate commerce or of the mails to offer to sell or offer to buy through the use or medium of any prospectus or otherwise any security, unless a registration statement has been filed as to such security, or while the registration statement is the subject of a refusal order or stop order or (prior to the effective date of the registration statement) any public proceeding or examination under section 8.

(d) LIMITATION.—Notwithstanding any other provision of this section, an emerging growth company or any person authorized to act on behalf of an emerging growth company may engage in oral or written communications with potential investors that are qualified institutional buyers or institutions that are accredited investors, as such terms are respectively defined in section 230.144A and section 230.501(a) of title 17, Code of Federal Regulations, or any successor thereto, to determine whether such investors might have an interest in a contemplated securities offering, either prior to or following the date of filing of a registration statement with respect to such securities with the Commission, subject to the requirement of subsection (b)(2).

(e) Notwithstanding the provisions of section 3 or 4, unless a registration statement meeting the requirements of section 10(a) is in effect as to a security-based swap, it shall be unlawful for any person, directly or indirectly, to make use of any means or instruments of transportation or communication in interstate commerce or of the mails to offer to sell, offer to buy or purchase or sell a security-based swap to any person who is not an eligible contract participant as defined in section 1a(18) of the Commodity Exchange Act (7 U.S.C. 1a(18)).

REGISTRATION OF SECURITIES AND SIGNING OF REGISTRATION STATEMENT

SEC. 6. [77f] (a) Any security may be registered with the Commission under the terms and conditions hereinafter provided, by filing a registration statement in triplicate, at least one of which shall be signed by each issuer, its principal executive officer or officers, its principal financial officer, its comptroller or principal accounting officer, and the majority of its board of directors or persons performing similar functions (or, if there is no board of directors or persons performing similar functions, by the majority of the persons or board having the power of management of the issuer), and in case the issuer is a foreign or Territorial person by its duly authorized representative in the United States; except that when such registration statement relates to a security issued by a foreign government, or political subdivision thereof, it need be signed only by the underwriter of such security. Signatures of all such persons when written on the said registration statements shall be presumed to have been so written by authority of the person whose signature is so affixed and the burden of proof, in the event such authority shall be denied, shall be upon the party denying the same. The affixing of any signature without the authority of the purported signer shall constitute a violation of this title. A registration statement shall be deemed effective only as to the securities specified therein as proposed to be offered.

(b) REGISTRATION FEE.—

(1) FEE PAYMENT REQUIRED.—At the time of filing a registration statement, the applicant shall pay to the Commission a fee at a rate that shall be equal to $92 per $1,000,000 of the maximum aggregate price at which such securities are proposed to be offered, except that during fiscal year 2003 and any succeeding fiscal year such fee shall be adjusted pursuant to paragraph (2).

(2) ANNUAL ADJUSTMENT.—For each fiscal year, the Commission shall by order adjust the rate required by paragraph (1) for such fiscal year to a rate that, when applied to the baseline estimate of the aggregate maximum offering prices for such fiscal year, is reasonably likely to produce aggregate fee collections under this subsection that are equal to the target fee collection amount for such fiscal year.

(3) PRO RATA APPLICATION.—The rates per $1,000,000 required by this subsection shall be applied pro rata to amounts and balances of less than $1,000,000.

(4) REVIEW AND EFFECTIVE DATE.—In exercising its authority under this subsection, the Commission shall not be required to comply with the provisions of section 553 of title 5, United States Code. An adjusted rate prescribed under paragraph (2) and published under paragraph (5) shall not be subject to judicial review. An adjusted rate prescribed under paragraph (2) shall take effect on the first day of the fiscal year to which such rate applies.

(5) PUBLICATION.—The Commission shall publish in the Federal Register notices of the rate applicable under this subsection and under sections 13(e) and 14(g) for each fiscal year not later than August 31 of the fiscal year preceding the fiscal year to which such rate applies, together with any estimates or projections on which such rate is based.

(6) DEFINITIONS.—For purposes of this subsection:

(A) TARGET OFFSETTING [19] COLLECTION AMOUNT.—The target fee collection amount for each fiscal year is determined according to the following table:

Fiscal year:	Target fee collection amount
2002	$377,000,000
2003	$435,000,000
2004	$467,000,000
2005	$570,000,000
2006	$689,000,000
2007	$214,000,000
2008	$234,000,000
2009	$284,000,000
2010	$334,000,000
2011	$394,000,000
2012	$425,000,000
2013	$455,000,000
2014	$485,000,000
2015	$515,000,000
2016	$550,000,000
2017	$585,000,000
2018	$620,000,000
2019	$660,000,000
2020	$705,000,000
2021 and each fiscal year thereafter	An amount that is equal to the target fee collection amount for the prior fiscal year, adjusted by the rate of inflation.

(B) BASELINE ESTIMATE OF THE AGGREGATE MAXIMUM OFFERING PRICES.—The baseline estimate of the aggregate maximum offering prices for any fiscal year is the baseline estimate of the aggregate maximum offering price at which securities are proposed to be offered pursuant to registration statements filed with the Commission during such fiscal year as determined by the Commission, after consultation with the Congressional Budget Office and the Office of Management and Budget, using the methodology required for projections pursuant to section 257 of the Balanced Budget and Emergency Deficit Control Act of 1985.

(c) The filing with the Commission of a registration statement, or of an amendment to a registration statement, shall be deemed to have taken place upon the receipt thereof, but the filing of a registration statement shall not be deemed to have taken place unless it is accompanied by a United States postal money order or a certified bank check or cash for the amount of the fee required under subsection (b).

(d) The information contained in or filed with any registration statement shall be made available to the public under such regulations as the Commission may prescribe, and copies thereof, photostatic or otherwise, shall be furnished to every applicant at such reasonable charge as the Commission may prescribe.

(e) EMERGING GROWTH COMPANIES.—

(1) IN GENERAL.—Any emerging growth company, prior to its initial public offering date, may confidentially submit to the Commission a draft registration statement, for confidential

---

[19] The word "OFFSETTING" in the heading of paragraph (6)(A) probably should read "FEE". See amendment made by section 991(b)(1)(A) of Public Law 111–203.

nonpublic review by the staff of the Commission prior to public filing, provided that the initial confidential submission and all amendments thereto shall be publicly filed with the Commission not later than 15 days before the date on which the issuer conducts a road show, as such term is defined in section 230.433(h)(4) of title 17, Code of Federal Regulations, or any successor thereto. An issuer that was an emerging growth company at the time it submitted a confidential registration statement or, in lieu thereof, a publicly filed registration statement for review under this subsection but ceases to be an emerging growth company thereafter shall continue to be treated as an emerging market growth company for the purposes of this subsection through the earlier of the date on which the issuer consummates its initial public offering pursuant to such registrations statement or the end of the 1-year period beginning on the date the company ceases to be an emerging growth company.

(2) CONFIDENTIALITY.—Notwithstanding any other provision of this title, the Commission shall not be compelled to disclose any information provided to or obtained by the Commission pursuant to this subsection. For purposes of section 552 of title 5, United States Code, this subsection shall be considered a statute described in subsection (b)(3)(B) of such section 552. Information described in or obtained pursuant to this subsection shall be deemed to constitute confidential information for purposes of section 24(b)(2) of the Securities Exchange Act of 1934.

INFORMATION REQUIRED IN REGISTRATION STATEMENT [20]

SEC. 7. [21] [77g]

(a) INFORMATION REQUIRED IN REGISTRATION STATEMENT.—

(1) IN GENERAL.—The registration statement, when relating to a security other than a security issued by a foreign government, or political subdivision thereof, shall contain the information, and be accompanied by the documents, specified in Schedule A, and when relating to a security issued by a foreign government, or political subdivision thereof, shall contain the information, and be accompanied by the documents, specified in Schedule B; except that the Commission may by rules or regulations provide that any such information or document need not be included in respect of any class of issuers or securities if it finds that the requirement of such information or document is inapplicable to such class and that disclosure fully adequate for the protection of investors is otherwise required to be included within the registration statement. If any accountant, engineer, or appraiser, or any person whose profession gives authority to a statement made by him, is named as having prepared or certified any part of the registration statement, or is named as having prepared or certified a report or valuation for use in connection with the registration statement, the written consent of such person shall be filed with the reg-

---

[20] But see sections 24(e) and 24(f) of the Investment Company Act of 1940, infra.
[21] For additional information required of certain public utilities, see 16 U.S.C. 824c(h).

istration statement. If any such person is named as having prepared or certified a report or valuation (other than a public official document or statement) which is used in connection with the registration statement, but is not named as having prepared or certified such report or valuation for use in connection with the registration statement, the written consent of such person shall be filed with the registration statement unless the Commission dispenses with such filing as impracticable or as involving undue hardship on the person filing the registration statement. Any such registration statement shall contain such other information, and be accompanied by such other documents, as the Commission may by rules or regulations require as being necessary or appropriate in the public interest or for the protection of investors.

(2) TREATMENT OF EMERGING GROWTH COMPANIES.—An emerging growth company—

(A) need not present more than 2 years of audited financial statements in order for the registration statement of such emerging growth company with respect to an initial public offering of its common equity securities to be effective, and in any other registration statement to be filed with the Commission, an emerging growth company need not present selected financial data in accordance with section 229.301 of title 17, Code of Federal Regulations, for any period prior to the earliest audited period presented in connection with its initial public offering; and

(B) may not be required to comply with any new or revised financial accounting standard until such date that a company that is not an issuer (as defined under section 2(a) of the Sarbanes-Oxley Act of 2002 (15 U.S.C. 7201(a))) is required to comply with such new or revised accounting standard, if such standard applies to companies that are not issuers.

(b)(1) The Commission shall prescribe special rules with respect to registration statements filed by any issuer that is a blank check company. Such rules may, as the Commission determines necessary or appropriate in the public interest or for the protection of investors—

(A) require such issuers to provide timely disclosure, prior to or after such statement becomes effective under section 8, of (i) information regarding the company to be acquired and the specific application of the proceeds of the offering, or (ii) additional information necessary to prevent such statement from being misleading;

(B) place limitations on the use of such proceeds and the distribution of securities by such issuer until the disclosures required under subparagraph (A) have been made; and

(C) provide a right of rescission to shareholders of such securities.

(2) The Commission may, as it determines consistent with the public interest and the protection of investors, by rule or order exempt any issuer or class of issuers from the rules prescribed under paragraph (1).

(3) For purposes of paragraph (1) of this subsection, the term "blank check company" means any development stage company that is issuing a penny stock (within the meaning of section 3(a)(51) of the Securities Exchange Act of 1934) and that—

(A) has no specific business plan or purpose; or

(B) has indicated that its business plan is to merge with an unidentified company or companies.

(c) DISCLOSURE REQUIREMENTS.—

(1) IN GENERAL.—The Commission shall adopt regulations under this subsection requiring each issuer of an asset-backed security to disclose, for each tranche or class of security, information regarding the assets backing that security.

(2) CONTENT OF REGULATIONS.—In adopting regulations under this subsection, the Commission shall—

(A) set standards for the format of the data provided by issuers of an asset-backed security, which shall, to the extent feasible, facilitate comparison of such data across securities in similar types of asset classes; and

(B) require issuers of asset-backed securities, at a minimum, to disclose asset-level or loan-level data, if such data are necessary for investors to independently perform due diligence, including—

(i) data having unique identifiers relating to loan brokers or originators;

(ii) the nature and extent of the compensation of the broker or originator of the assets backing the security; and

(iii) the amount of risk retention by the originator and the securitizer of such assets.

(d) REGISTRATION STATEMENT FOR ASSET-BACKED SECURITIES.—Not later than 180 days after the date of enactment of this subsection, the Commission shall issue rules relating to the registration statement required to be filed by any issuer of an asset-backed security (as that term is defined in section 3(a)(77) of the Securities Exchange Act of 1934) that require any issuer of an asset-backed security—

(1) to perform a review of the assets underlying the asset-backed security; and

(2) to disclose the nature of the review under paragraph (1).

TAKING EFFECT OF REGISTRATION STATEMENTS AND AMENDMENTS THERETO

SEC. 8. [77h] (a) Except as hereinafter provided, the effective date of a registration statement shall be the twentieth day after the filing thereof or such earlier date as the Commission may determine, having due regard to the adequacy of the information respecting the issuer theretofore available to the public, to the facility with which the nature of the securities to be registered, their relationship to the capital structure of the issuer and the rights of holders thereof can be understood, and to the public interest and the protection of investors. If any amendment to any such statement is filed prior to the effective date of such statement, the registration statement shall be deemed to have been filed when such amendment was filed; except that an amendment filed with the consent of the Commission, prior to the effective date of the registration statement, or filed pursuant to an order of the Commission, shall be treated as a part of the registration statement.

(b) If it appears to the Commission that a registration statement is on its face incomplete or inaccurate in any material respect, the Commission may, after notice by personal service or the sending of confirmed telegraphic notice not later than ten days after the filing of the registration statement, and opportunity for hearing (at a time fixed by the Commission) within ten days after such notice by personal service or the sending of such telegraphic notice, issue an order prior to the effective date of registration refusing to permit such statement to become effective until it has been amended in accordance with such order. When such statement has been amended in accordance with such order the Commission shall so declare and the registration shall become effective at the time provided in subsection (a) or upon the date of such declaration, whichever date is the later.

(c) An amendment filed after the effective date of the registration statement, if such amendment, upon its face, appears to the Commission not to be incomplete or inaccurate in any material respect, shall become effective on such date as the Commission may determine, having due regard to the public interest and the protection of investors.

(d) If it appears to the Commission at any time that the registration statement includes any untrue statement of a material fact or omits to state any material fact required to be stated therein or necessary to make the statements therein not misleading, the Commission may, after notice by personal service or the sending of confirmed telegraphic notice, and after opportunity for hearing (at a time fixed by the Commission) within fifteen days after such notice by personal service or the sending of such telegraphic notice, issue a stop order suspending the effectiveness of the registration statement.[22] When such statement has been amended in accordance with such stop order the Commission shall so declare and thereupon the stop order shall cease to be effective.

(e) The Commission is hereby empowered to make an examination in any case in order to determine whether a stop order should issue under subsection (d). In making such examination the Commission or any officer or officers designated by it shall have access to and may demand the production of any books and papers of, and may administer oaths and affirmations to and examine, the issuer, underwriter, or any other person, in respect of any matter relevant to the examination, and may, in its discretion, require the production of a balance sheet exhibiting the assets and liabilities of the issuer, or its income statement, or both, to be certified to by a public or certified accountant approved by the Commission. If the issuer or underwriter shall fail to cooperate, or shall obstruct or refuse to permit the making of an examination, such conduct shall be proper ground for the issuance of a stop order.

---

[22] See also section 14(a) of the Investment Company Act of 1940, infra.

(f) Any notice required under this section shall be sent to or served on the issuer, or, in case of a foreign government or political subdivision thereof, to or on the underwriter, or, in the case of a foreign or Territorial person, to or on its duly authorized representative in the United States named in the registration statement, properly directed in each case of telegraphic notice to the address given in such statement.

CEASE-AND-DESIST PROCEEDINGS

SEC. 8A. [77h-1] (a) AUTHORITY OF THE COMMISSION.—If the Commission finds, after notice and opportunity for hearing, that any person is violating, has violated, or is about to violate any provision of this title, or any rule or regulation thereunder, the Commission may publish its findings and enter an order requiring such person, and any other person that is, was, or would be a cause of the violation, due to an act or omission the person knew or should have known would contribute to such violation, to cease and desist from committing or causing such violation and any future violation of the same provision, rule, or regulation. Such order may, in addition to requiring a person to cease and desist from committing or causing a violation, require such person to comply, or to take steps to effect compliance, with such provision, rule, or regulation, upon such terms and conditions and within such time as the Commission may specify in such order. Any such order may, as the Commission deems appropriate, require future compliance or steps to effect future compliance, either permanently or for such period of time as the Commission may specify, with such provision, rule, or regulation with respect to any security, any issuer, or any other person.

(b) HEARING.—The notice instituting proceedings pursuant to subsection (a) shall fix a hearing date not earlier than 30 days nor later than 60 days after service of the notice unless an earlier or a later date is set by the Commission with the consent of any respondent so served.

(c) TEMPORARY ORDER.—

(1) IN GENERAL.—Whenever the Commission determines that the alleged violation or threatened violation specified in the notice instituting proceedings pursuant to subsection (a), or the continuation thereof, is likely to result in significant dissipation or conversion of assets, significant harm to investors, or substantial harm to the public interest, including, but not limited to, losses to the Securities Investor Protection Corporation, prior to the completion of the proceedings, the Commission may enter a temporary order requiring the respondent to cease and desist from the violation or threatened violation and to take such action to prevent the violation or threatened violation and to prevent dissipation or conversion of assets, significant harm to investors, or substantial harm to the public interest as the Commission deems appropriate pending completion of such proceeding. Such an order shall be entered only after notice and opportunity for a hearing, unless the Commission determines that notice and hearing prior to entry would be impracticable or contrary to the public interest. A temporary order shall become effective upon service upon the respondent and, unless set aside, limited, or suspended by the Commission

or a court of competent jurisdiction, shall remain effective and enforceable pending the completion of the proceedings.

(2) APPLICABILITY.—This subsection shall apply only to a respondent that acts, or, at the time of the alleged misconduct acted, as a broker, dealer, investment adviser, investment company, municipal securities dealer, government securities broker, government securities dealer, or transfer agent, or is, or was at the time of the alleged misconduct, an associated person of, or a person seeking to become associated with, any of the foregoing.

(d) REVIEW OF TEMPORARY ORDERS.—

(1) COMMISSION REVIEW.—At any time after the respondent has been served with a temporary cease-and-desist order pursuant to subsection (c), the respondent may apply to the Commission to have the order set aside, limited, or suspended. If the respondent has been served with a temporary cease-and-desist order entered without a prior Commission hearing, the respondent may, within 10 days after the date on which the order was served, request a hearing on such application and the Commission shall hold a hearing and render a decision on such application at the earliest possible time.

(2) JUDICIAL REVIEW.—Within—

(A) 10 days after the date the respondent was served with a temporary cease-and-desist order entered with a prior Commission hearing, or

(B) 10 days after the Commission renders a decision on an application and hearing under paragraph (1), with respect to any temporary cease-and-desist order entered without a prior Commission hearing,

the respondent may apply to the United States district court for the district in which the respondent resides or has its principal place of business, or for the District of Columbia, for an order setting aside, limiting, or suspending the effectiveness or enforcement of the order, and the court shall have jurisdiction to enter such an order. A respondent served with a temporary cease-and-desist order entered without a prior Commission hearing may not apply to the court except after hearing and decision by the Commission on the respondent's application under paragraph (1) of this subsection.

(3) NO AUTOMATIC STAY OF TEMPORARY ORDER.—The commencement of proceedings under paragraph (2) of this subsection shall not, unless specifically ordered by the court, operate as a stay of the Commission's order.

(4) EXCLUSIVE REVIEW.—Section 9(a) of this title shall not apply to a temporary order entered pursuant to this section.

(e) AUTHORITY TO ENTER AN ORDER REQUIRING AN ACCOUNTING AND DISGORGEMENT.—In any cease-and-desist proceeding under subsection (a), the Commission may enter an order requiring accounting and disgorgement, including reasonable interest. The Commission is authorized to adopt rules, regulations, and orders concerning payments to investors, rates of interest, periods of accrual, and such other matters as it deems appropriate to implement this subsection.

(f) AUTHORITY OF THE COMMISSION TO PROHIBIT PERSONS FROM SERVING AS OFFICERS OR DIRECTORS.—In any cease-and-desist proceeding under subsection (a), the Commission may issue an order to prohibit, conditionally or unconditionally, and permanently or for such period of time as it shall determine, any person who has violated section 17(a)(1) or the rules or regulations thereunder, from acting as an officer or director of any issuer that has a class of securities registered pursuant to section 12 of the Securities Exchange Act of 1934, or that is required to file reports pursuant to section 15(d) of that Act, if the conduct of that person demonstrates unfitness to serve as an officer or director of any such issuer.

(g) AUTHORITY TO IMPOSE MONEY PENALTIES.—

(1) GROUNDS.—In any cease-and-desist proceeding under subsection (a), the Commission may impose a civil penalty on a person if the Commission finds, on the record, after notice and opportunity for hearing, that—

(A) such person—

(i) is violating or has violated any provision of this title, or any rule or regulation issued under this title; or

(ii) is or was a cause of the violation of any provision of this title, or any rule or regulation thereunder; and

(B) such penalty is in the public interest.

(2) MAXIMUM AMOUNT OF PENALTY.—

(A) FIRST TIER.—The maximum amount of a penalty for each act or omission described in paragraph (1) shall be $7,500 for a natural person or $75,000 for any other person.

(B) SECOND TIER.—Notwithstanding subparagraph (A), the maximum amount of penalty for each such act or omission shall be $75,000 for a natural person or $375,000 for any other person, if the act or omission described in paragraph (1) involved fraud, deceit, manipulation, or deliberate or reckless disregard of a regulatory requirement.

(C) THIRD TIER.—Notwithstanding subparagraphs (A) and (B), the maximum amount of penalty for each such act or omission shall be $150,000 for a natural person or $725,000 for any other person, if—

(i) the act or omission described in paragraph (1) involved fraud, deceit, manipulation, or deliberate or reckless disregard of a regulatory requirement; and

(ii) such act or omission directly or indirectly resulted in—

(I) substantial losses or created a significant risk of substantial losses to other persons; or

(II) substantial pecuniary gain to the person who committed the act or omission.

(3) EVIDENCE CONCERNING ABILITY TO PAY.—In any proceeding in which the Commission may impose a penalty under this section, a respondent may present evidence of the ability of the respondent to pay such penalty. The Commission may, in its discretion, consider such evidence in determining whether such penalty is in the public interest. Such evidence may re-

late to the extent of the ability of the respondent to continue in business and the collectability of a penalty, taking into account any other claims of the United States or third parties upon the assets of the respondent and the amount of the assets of the respondent.

COURT REVIEW OF ORDERS

SEC. 9. [77i] (a) Any person aggrieved by an order of the Commission may obtain a review of such order in the court of appeals of the United States, within any circuit wherein such person resides or has his principal place of business, or in the United States Court of Appeals for the District of Columbia, by filing in such Court; within sixty days after the entry of such order, a written petition praying that the order of the Commission be modified or be set aside in whole or in part. A copy of such petition shall be forthwith transmitted by the clerk of the court to the Commission, and thereupon the Commission shall file in the court the record upon which the order complained of was entered, as provided in section 2112 of title 28, United States Code. No objection to the order of the Commission shall be considered by the court unless such objection shall have been urged before the Commission. The finding of the Commission as to the facts, if supported by evidence, shall be conclusive. If either party shall apply to the court for leave to adduce additional evidence, and shall show to the satisfaction of the court that such additional evidence is material and that there were reasonable grounds for failure to adduce such evidence in the hearing before the Commission, the court may order such additional evidence to be taken before the Commission and to be adduced upon the hearing in such manner and upon such terms and conditions as to the court may seem proper. The Commission may modify its findings as to the facts, by reason of the additional evidence so taken, and it shall file such modified or new findings, which, if supported by evidence, shall be conclusive, and its recommendation, if any, for the modification or setting aside of the original order. The jurisdiction of the court shall be exclusive and its judgment and decree, affirming, modifying, or setting aside, in whole or in part, any order of the Commission, shall be final, subject to review by the Supreme Court of the United States upon certiorari or certification as provided in section 1254 of title 28, United States Code.

(b) The commencement of proceedings under subsection (a) shall not, unless specifically ordered by the court, operate as a stay of the Commission's order.

INFORMATION REQUIRED IN PROSPECTUS

SEC. 10. [77j] (a) Except to the extent otherwise permitted or required pursuant to this subsection or subsections (c), (d), or (e)—
(1) a prospectus relating to a security other than a security issued by a foreign government or political subdivision thereof, shall contain the information contained in the registration statement, but it need not include the documents referred to in paragraphs (28) to (32), inclusive, of schedule A;

(2) a prospectus relating to a security issued by a foreign government or political subdivision thereof shall contain the information contained in the registration statement, but it need not include the documents referred to in paragraphs (13) and (14) of schedule B;

(3) notwithstanding the provisions of paragraphs (1) and (2) of this subsection (a) when a prospectus is used more than nine months after the effective date of the registration statement, the information contained therein shall be as of a date not more than sixteen months prior to such use, so far as such information is known to the user of such prospectus or can be furnished by such user without unreasonable effort or expense;[23]

(4) there may be omitted from any prospectus any of the information required under this subsection (a) which the Commission may by rules or regulations designate as not being necessary or appropriate in the public interest or for the protection of investors.

(b) In addition to the prospectus permitted or required in subsection (a), the Commission shall by rules or regulations deemed necessary or appropriate in the public interest or for the protection of investors permit the use of a prospectus for the purposes of subsection (b)(1) of section 5 which omits in part or summarizes information in the prospectus specified in subsection (a). A prospectus permitted under this subsection shall, except to the extent the Commission by rules or regulations deemed necessary or appropriate in the public interest or for the protection of investors otherwise provides, be filed as part of the registration statement but shall not be deemed a part of such registration statement for the purposes of section 11. The Commission may at any time issue an order preventing or suspending the use of a prospectus permitted under this subsection (b), if it has reason to believe that such prospectus has not been filed (if required to be filed as part of the registration statement) or includes any untrue statement of a material fact or omits to state any material fact required to be stated therein or necessary to make the statements therein, in the light of the circumstances under which such prospectus is or is to be used, not misleading. Upon issuance of an order under this subsection, the Commission shall give notice of the issuance of such order and opportunity for hearing by personal service or the sending of confirmed telegraphic notice. The Commission shall vacate or modify the order at any time for good cause or if such prospectus has been filed or amended in accordance with such order.

(c) Any prospectus shall contain such other information as the Commission may by rules or regulations require as being necessary or appropriate in the public interest or for the protection of investors.

(d) In the exercise of its powers under subsections (a), (b), or (c), the Commission shall have authority to classify prospectuses according to the nature and circumstances of their use or the nature of the security, issue, issuer, or otherwise, and, by rules and regulations and subject to such terms and conditions as it shall

---

[23] See also section 24(e) of the Investment Company Act of 1940, infra.

specify therein, to prescribe as to each class the form and contents which it may find appropriate and consistent with the public interest and the protection of investors.

(e) The statements or information required to be included in a prospectus by or under authority of subsections (a), (b), (c), or (d), when written, shall be placed in a conspicuous part of the prospectus and, except as otherwise permitted by rules or regulations, in type as large as that used generally in the body of the prospectus.

(f) In any case where a prospectus consists of a radio or television broadcast, copies thereof shall be filed with the Commission under such rules and regulations as it shall prescribe. The Commission may by rules and regulations require the filing with it of forms and prospectuses used in connection with the offer or sale of securities registered under this title.

CIVIL LIABILITIES ON ACCOUNT OF FALSE REGISTRATION STATEMENT

SEC. 11. [77k] (a) In case any part of the registration statement, when such part became effective,[24] contained an untrue statement of a material fact or omitted to state a material fact required to be stated therein or necessary to make the statements therein not misleading, any person acquiring such security (unless it is proved that at the time of such acquisition he knew of such untruth or omission) may, either at law or in equity, in any court of competent jurisdiction, sue—

    (1) every person who signed the registration statement;

    (2) every person who was a director of (or person performing similar functions) or partner in, the issuer at the time of the filing of the part of the registration statement with respect to which his liability is asserted;

    (3) every person who, with his consent, is named in the registration statement as being or about to become a director, person performing similar functions or partner;

    (4) every accountant, engineer, or appraiser, or any person whose profession gives authority to a statement made by him, who has with his consent been named as having prepared or certified any part of the registration statement, or as having prepared or certified any report or valuation which is used in connection with the registration statement, with respect to the statement in such registration statement, report, or valuation, which purports to have been prepared or certified by him;

    (5) every underwriter with respect to such security.

If such person acquired the security after the issuer has made generally available to its security holders an earning statement covering a period of at least twelve months beginning after the effective date of the registration statement, then the right of recovery under this subsection shall be conditioned on proof that such person acquired the security relying upon such untrue statement in the registration statement or relying upon the registration statement and not knowing of such omission, but such reliance may be established without proof of the reading of the registration statement by such person.

---

[24] See also section 24(e) of the Investment Company Act of 1940, infra.

(b) Notwithstanding the provisions of subsection (a) no person, other than the issuer, shall be liable as provided therein who shall sustain the burden of proof—

(1) that before the effective date of the part of the registration statement with respect to which his liability is asserted (A) he had resigned from or had taken such steps as are permitted by law to resign from, or ceased or refused to act in, every office, capacity, or relationship in which he was described in the registration statement as acting or agreeing to act, and (B) he had advised the Commission and the issuer in writing that he had taken such action and that he would not be responsible for such part of the registration statement; or

(2) that if such part of the registration statement became effective without his knowledge, upon becoming aware of such fact he forthwith acted and advised the Commission, in accordance with paragraph (1), and, in addition, gave reasonable public notice that such part of the registration statement had become effective without his knowledge; or

(3) that (A) as regards any part of the registration statement not purporting to be made on the authority of an expert, and not purporting to be a copy of or extract from a report or valuation of an expert, and not purporting to be made on the authority of a public official document or statement, he had, after reasonable investigation, reasonable ground to believe and did believe, at the time such part of the registration statement became effective, that the statements therein were true and that there was no omission to state a material fact required to be stated therein or necessary to make the statements therein not misleading; and (B) as regards any part of the registration statement purporting to be made upon his authority as an expert or purporting to be a copy of or extract from a report or valuation of himself as an expert, (i) he had, after reasonable investigation, reasonable ground to believe and did believe, at the time such part of the registration statement became effective, that the statements therein were true and that there was no omission to state a material fact required to be stated therein or necessary to make the statements therein not misleading, or (ii) such part of the registration statement did not fairly represent his statement as an expert or was not a fair copy of or extract from his report or valuation as an expert; and (C) as regards any part of the registration statement purporting to be made on the authority of an expert (other than himself) or purporting to be a copy of or extract from a report or valuation of an expert (other than himself), he had no reasonable ground to believe and did not believe, at the time such part of the registration statement became effective, that the statements therein were untrue or that there was an omission to state a material fact required to be stated therein or necessary to make the statements therein not misleading, or that such part of the registration statement did not fairly represent the statement of the expert or was not a fair copy of or extract from the report or valuation of the expert; and (D) as regards any part of the registration statement purporting to be a statement made by an official person or pur-

Sec. 11 **SECURITIES ACT OF 1933**

porting to be a copy of or extract from a public official document, he had no reasonable ground to believe and did not believe, at the time such part of the registration statement became effective, that the statements therein were untrue, or that there was an ommission to state a material fact required to be stated therein or necessary to make the statements therein not misleading, or that such part of the registration statement did not fairly represent the statement made by the official person or was not a fair copy of or extract from the public official document.

(c) In determining, for the purpose of paragraph (3) of subsection (b) of this section, what constitutes reasonable investigation and reasonable ground for belief, the standard of reasonableness shall be that required of a prudent man in the management of his own property.

(d) If any person becomes an underwriter with respect to the security after the part of the registration statement with respect to which his liability is asserted has become effective, then for the purposes of paragraph (3) of subsection (b) of this section such part of the registration statement shall be considered as having become effective with respect to such person as of the time when he became an underwriter.

(e) The suit authorized under subsection (a) may be to recover such damages as shall represent the difference between the amount paid for the security (not exceeding the price at which the security was offered to the public) and (1) the value thereof as of the time such suit was brought, or (2) the price at which such security shall have been disposed of in the market before suit, or (3) the price at which such security shall have been disposed of after suit but before judgment if such damages shall be less than the damages representing the difference between the amount paid for the security (not exceeding the price at which the security was offered to the public) and the value thereof as of the time such suit was brought: *Provided,* That if the defendant proves that any portion or all of such damages represents other than the depreciation in value of such security resulting from such part of the registration statement, with respect to which his liability is asserted, not being true or omitting to state a material fact required to be stated therein or necessary to make the statements therein not misleading, such portion of or all such damages shall not be recoverable. In no event shall any underwriter (unless such underwriter shall have knowingly received from the issuer for acting as an underwriter some benefit, directly or indirectly, in which all other underwriters similarly situated did not share in proportion to their respective interests in the underwriting) be liable in any suit or as a consequence of suits authorized under subsection (a) for damages in excess of the total price at which the securities underwritten by him and distributed to the public were offered to the public. In any suit under this or any other section of this title the court may, in its discretion, require an undertaking for the payment of the costs of such suit, including reasonable attorney's fees, and if judgment shall be rendered against a party litigant, upon the motion of the other party litigant, such costs may be assessed in favor of such party litigant (whether or not such undertaking has been required) if the court believes the suit or the defense to have been without merit, in an amount sufficient to reimburse him for the reasonable expenses incurred by him, in connection with such suit, such costs to be taxed in the manner usually provided for taxing of costs in the court in which the suit was heard.

(f)(1) Except as provided in paragraph (2), all or any one or more of the persons specified in subsection (a) shall be jointly and severally liable, and every person who becomes liable to make any payment under this section may recover contribution as in cases of contract from any person who, if sued separately, would have been liable to make the same payment, unless the person who has become liable was, and the other was not, guilty of fraudulent misrepresentation.

(2)(A) The liability of an outside director under subsection (e) shall be determined in accordance with section 21D(f) of the Securities Exchange Act of 1934.

(B) For purposes of this paragraph, the term "outside director" shall have the meaning given such term by rule or regulation of the Commission.

(g) In no case shall the amount recoverable under this section exceed the price at which the security was offered to the public.

CIVIL LIABILITIES ARISING IN CONNECTION WITH PROSPECTUSES AND COMMUNICATIONS

SEC. 12. [77l] (a) IN GENERAL.—Any person who—
    (1) offers or sells a security in violation of section 5, or
    (2) offers or sells a security (whether or not exempted by the provisions of section 3, other than paragraphs (2) and (14) of subsection (a) thereof), by the use of any means or instruments of transportation or communication in interstate commerce or of the mails, by means of a prospectus or oral communication, which includes an untrue statement of a material fact or omits to state a material fact necessary in order to make the statements, in the light of the circumstances under which they were made, not misleading (the purchaser not knowing of such untruth or omission), and who shall not sustain the burden of proof that he did not know, and in the exercise of reasonable care could not have known, of such untruth or omission,
shall be liable, subject to subsection (b), to the person purchasing such security from him, who may sue either at law or in equity in any court of competent jurisdiction, to recover the consideration paid for such security with interest thereon, less the amount of any income received thereon, upon the tender of such security, or for damages if he no longer owns the security.

(b) LOSS CAUSATION.—In an action described in subsection (a)(2), if the person who offered or sold such security proves that any portion or all of the amount recoverable under subsection (a)(2) represents other than the depreciation in value of the subject security resulting from such part of the prospectus or oral communication, with respect to which the liability of that person is asserted, not being true or omitting to state a material fact required to be stated therein or necessary to make the statement not misleading, then such portion or amount, as the case may be, shall not be recoverable.

LIMITATION OF ACTIONS

SEC. 13. [77m] No action shall be maintained to enforce any liability created under section 11 or section 12(a)(2) unless brought within one year after the discovery of the untrue statement or the omission, or after such discovery should have been made by the exercise of reasonable diligence, or, if the action is to enforce a liability created under section 12(a)(1), unless brought within one year after the violation upon which it is based. In no event shall any such action be brought to enforce a liability created under section 11 or section 12(a)(1) more than three years after the security was bona fide offered to the public, or under section 12(a)(2) more than three years after the sale.[25]

CONTRARY STIPULATIONS VOID

SEC. 14. [77n] Any condition, stipulation, or provision binding any person acquiring any security to waive compliance with any provision of this title or of the rules and regulations of the Commission shall be void.

LIABILITY OF CONTROLLING PERSONS

SEC. 15. [77o] (a) CONTROLLING PERSONS.—Every person who, by or through stock ownership, agency, or otherwise, or who, pursuant to or in connection with an agreement or understanding with one or more other persons by or through stock ownership, agency, or otherwise, controls any person liable under section 11 or 12, shall also be liable jointly and severally with and to the same extent as such controlled person to any person to whom such controlled person is liable, unless the controlling person had no knowledge of or reasonable ground to believe in the existence of the facts by reason of which the liability of the controlled person is alleged to exist.

(b) PROSECUTION OF PERSONS WHO AID AND ABET VIOLATIONS.—For purposes of any action brought by the Commission under subparagraph (b) or (d) of section 20, any person that knowingly or recklessly provides substantial assistance to another person in violation of a provision of this Act, or of any rule or regulation issued under this Act, shall be deemed to be in violation of such provision to the same extent as the person to whom such assistance is provided.

SEC. 16. [77p] ADDITIONAL REMEDIES; LIMITATION ON REMEDIES.[26]

(a) REMEDIES ADDITIONAL.—Except as provided in subsection (b), the rights and remedies provided by this title shall be in addi-

---

[25] See also section 24(e) of the Investment Company Act of 1940, infra.
[26] Section 16 of the Securities Act of 1933 was amended to add limitations on remedies by section 101 of the Securities Litigation Uniform Standards Act of 1998. Section 2 of that Act contained the following findings:

SEC. 2. FINDINGS.
The Congress finds that—

tion to any and all other rights and remedies that may exist at law or in equity.

(b) CLASS ACTION LIMITATIONS.—No covered class action based upon the statutory or common law of any State or subdivision thereof may be maintained in any State or Federal court by any private party alleging—

(1) an untrue statement or omission of a material fact in connection with the purchase or sale of a covered security; or

(2) that the defendant used or employed any manipulative or deceptive device or contrivance in connection with the purchase or sale of a covered security.

(c) REMOVAL OF COVERED CLASS ACTIONS.—Any covered class action brought in any State court involving a covered security, as set forth in subsection (b), shall be removable to the Federal district court for the district in which the action is pending, and shall be subject to subsection (b).

(d) PRESERVATION OF CERTAIN ACTIONS.—

(1) ACTIONS UNDER STATE LAW OF STATE OF INCORPORATION.—

(A) ACTIONS PRESERVED.—Notwithstanding subsection (b) or (c), a covered class action described in subparagraph (B) of this paragraph that is based upon the statutory or common law of the State in which the issuer is incorporated (in the case of a corporation) or organized (in the case of any other entity) may be maintained in a State or Federal court by a private party.

---

(1) the Private Securities Litigation Reform Act of 1995 sought to prevent abuses in private securities fraud lawsuits;

(2) since enactment of that legislation, considerable evidence has been presented to Congress that a number of securities class action lawsuits have shifted from Federal to State courts;

(3) this shift has prevented that Act from fully achieving its objectives;

(4) State securities regulation is of continuing importance, together with Federal regulation of securities, to protect investors and promote strong financial markets; and

(5) in order to prevent certain State private securities class action lawsuits alleging fraud from being used to frustrate the objectives of the Private Securities Litigation Reform Act of 1995, it is appropriate to enact national standards for securities class action lawsuits involving nationally traded securities, while preserving the appropriate enforcement powers of State securities regulators and not changing the current treatment of individual lawsuits.

Section 101(c) of that Act contained the following effective date provision for the amendment to section 16 of the Securities Act of 1933 and section 28(f) of the Securities Exchange Act of 1934:

(c) APPLICABILITY.—The amendments made by this section shall not affect or apply to any action commenced before and pending on the date of enactment of this Act.

In addition, section 102 of the Securities Litigation Uniform Standards Act contained the following provision with respect to reciprocal subpoena enforcement:

SEC. 102. PROMOTION OF RECIPROCAL SUBPOENA ENFORCEMENT.

(a) COMMISSION ACTION.—The Securities and Exchange Commission, in consultation with State securities commissions (or any agencies or offices performing like functions), shall seek to encourage the adoption of State laws providing for reciprocal enforcement by State securities commissions of subpoenas issued by another State securities commission seeking to compel persons to attend, testify in, or produce documents or records in connection with an action or investigation by a State securities commission of an alleged violation of State securities laws.

(b) REPORT.—Not later than 24 months after the date of enactment of this Act, the Securities and Exchange Commission (hereafter in this section referred to as the "Commission") shall submit a report to the Congress—

(1) identifying the States that have adopted laws described in subsection (a);

(2) describing the actions undertaken by the Commission and State securities commissions to promote the adoption of such laws; and

(3) identifying any further actions that the Commission recommends for such purposes.

(B) PERMISSIBLE ACTIONS.—A covered class action is described in this subparagraph if it involves—
 (i) the purchase or sale of securities by the issuer or an affiliate of the issuer exclusively from or to holders of equity securities of the issuer; or
 (ii) any recommendation, position, or other communication with respect to the sale of securities of the issuer that—
  (I) is made by or on behalf of the issuer or an affiliate of the issuer to holders of equity securities of the issuer; and
  (II) concerns decisions of those equity holders with respect to voting their securities, acting in response to a tender or exchange offer, or exercising dissenters' or appraisal rights.

(2) STATE ACTIONS.—
 (A) IN GENERAL.—Notwithstanding any other provision of this section, nothing in this section may be construed to preclude a State or political subdivision thereof or a State pension plan from bringing an action involving a covered security on its own behalf, or as a member of a class comprised solely of other States, political subdivisions, or State pension plans that are named plaintiffs, and that have authorized participation, in such action.
 (B) STATE PENSION PLAN DEFINED.—For purposes of this paragraph, the term "State pension plan" means a pension plan established and maintained for its employees by the government of the State or political subdivision thereof, or by any agency or instrumentality thereof.

(3) ACTIONS UNDER CONTRACTUAL AGREEMENTS BETWEEN ISSUERS AND INDENTURE TRUSTEES.—Notwithstanding subsection (b) or (c), a covered class action that seeks to enforce a contractual agreement between an issuer and an indenture trustee may be maintained in a State or Federal court by a party to the agreement or a successor to such party.

(4) REMAND OF REMOVED ACTIONS.—In an action that has been removed from a State court pursuant to subsection (c), if the Federal court determines that the action may be maintained in State court pursuant to this subsection, the Federal court shall remand such action to such State court.

(e) PRESERVATION OF STATE JURISDICTION.—The securities commission (or any agency or office performing like functions) of any State shall retain jurisdiction under the laws of such State to investigate and bring enforcement actions.

(f) DEFINITIONS.—For purposes of this section, the following definitions shall apply:
 (1) AFFILIATE OF THE ISSUER.—The term "affiliate of the issuer" means a person that directly or indirectly, through one or more intermediaries, controls or is controlled by or is under common control with, the issuer.
 (2) COVERED CLASS ACTION.—
  (A) IN GENERAL.—The term "covered class action" means—
   (i) any single lawsuit in which—

(I) damages are sought on behalf of more than 50 persons or prospective class members, and questions of law or fact common to those persons or members of the prospective class, without reference to issues of individualized reliance on an alleged misstatement or omission, predominate over any questions affecting only individual persons or members; or

(II) one or more named parties seek to recover damages on a representative basis on behalf of themselves and other unnamed parties similarly situated, and questions of law or fact common to those persons or members of the prospective class predominate over any questions affecting only individual persons or members; or

(ii) any group of lawsuits filed in or pending in the same court and involving common questions of law or fact, in which—

(I) damages are sought on behalf of more than 50 persons; and

(II) the lawsuits are joined, consolidated, or otherwise proceed as a single action for any purpose.

(B) EXCEPTION FOR DERIVATIVE ACTIONS.—Notwithstanding subparagraph (A), the term "covered class action" does not include an exclusively derivative action brought by one or more shareholders on behalf of a corporation.

(C) COUNTING OF CERTAIN CLASS MEMBERS.—For purposes of this paragraph, a corporation, investment company, pension plan, partnership, or other entity, shall be treated as one person or prospective class member, but only if the entity is not established for the purpose of participating in the action.

(D) RULE OF CONSTRUCTION.—Nothing in this paragraph shall be construed to affect the discretion of a State court in determining whether actions filed in such court should be joined, consolidated, or otherwise allowed to proceed as a single action.

(3) COVERED SECURITY.—The term "covered security" means a security that satisfies the standards for a covered security specified in paragraph (1) or (2) of section 18(b) at the time during which it is alleged that the misrepresentation, omission, or manipulative or deceptive conduct occurred, except that such term shall not include any debt security that is exempt from registration under this title pursuant to rules issued by the Commission under section 4(2).

FRAUDULENT INTERSTATE TRANSACTIONS

SEC. 17. [77q] (a) It shall be unlawful for any person in the offer or sale of any securities (including security-based swaps) or any security-based swap agreement (as defined in section 3(a)(78) of the Securities Exchange Act[27]) by the use of any means or instruments of transportation or communication in interstate commerce or by use of the mails, directly or indirectly—

(1) to employ any device, scheme, or artifice to defraud, or

(2) to obtain money or property by means of any untrue statement of a material fact or any omission to state a material fact necessary in order to make the statements made, in light of the circumstances under which they were made, not misleading; or

(3) to engage in any transaction, practice, or course of business which operates or would operate as a fraud or deceit upon the purchaser.

(b) It shall be unlawful for any person, by the use of any means or instruments of transportation or communication in interstate commerce or by the use of the mails, to publish, give publicity to, or circulate any notice, circular, advertisement, newspaper, article, letter, investment service, or communication which, though not purporting to offer a security for sale, describes such security for a consideration received or to be received, directly or indirectly, from an issuer, underwriter, or dealer, without fully disclosing the receipt, whether past or prospective, of such consideration and the amount thereof.

(c) The exemptions provided in section 3 shall not apply to the provisions of this section.

(d) The authority of the Commission under this section with respect to security-based swap agreements (as defined in section 3(a)(78) of the Securities Exchange Act of 1934) shall be subject to the restrictions and limitations of section 2A(b) of this title.

SEC. 18. [77r] EXEMPTION FROM STATE REGULATION OF SECURITIES OFFERINGS.

(a) SCOPE OF EXEMPTION.—Except as otherwise provided in this section, no law, rule, regulation, or order, or other administrative action of any State or any political subdivision thereof—

(1) requiring, or with respect to, registration or qualification of securities, or registration or qualification of securities transactions, shall directly or indirectly apply to a security that—

(A) is a covered security; or

(B) will be a covered security upon completion of the transaction;

(2) shall directly or indirectly prohibit, limit, or impose any conditions upon the use of—

(A) with respect to a covered security described in subsection (b), any offering document that is prepared by or on behalf of the issuer; or

(B) any proxy statement, report to shareholders, or other disclosure document relating to a covered security or the issuer thereof that is required to be and is filed with the Commission or any national securities organization registered under section 15A of the Securities Exchange Act of 1934, except that this subparagraph does not apply

---

[27] The reference in the matter preceding paragraph (1) to the "Securities Exchange Act" probably should read "Securities Exchange Act of 1934".

to the laws, rules, regulations, or orders, or other administrative actions of the State of incorporation of the issuer; or

(3) shall directly or indirectly prohibit, limit, or impose conditions, based on the merits of such offering or issuer, upon the offer or sale of any security described in paragraph (1).

(b) COVERED SECURITIES.—For purposes of this section, the following are covered securities:

(1) EXCLUSIVE FEDERAL REGISTRATION OF NATIONALLY TRADED SECURITIES.—A security is a covered security if such security is—

(A) a security designated as qualified for trading in the national market system pursuant to section 11A(a)(2) of the Securities Exchange Act of 1934 (15 U.S.C. 78k–1(a)(2)) that is listed, or authorized for listing, on a national securities exchange (or tier or segment thereof); or

(B) a security of the same issuer that is equal in seniority or that is a senior security to a security described in subparagraph (A).

(2) EXCLUSIVE FEDERAL REGISTRATION OF INVESTMENT COMPANIES.—A security is a covered security if such security is a security issued by an investment company that is registered, or that has filed a registration statement, under the Investment Company Act of 1940.

(3) SALES TO QUALIFIED PURCHASERS.—A security is a covered security with respect to the offer or sale of the security to qualified purchasers, as defined by the Commission by rule. In prescribing such rule, the Commission may define the term "qualified purchaser" differently with respect to different categories of securities, consistent with the public interest and the protection of investors.

(4) EXEMPTION IN CONNECTION WITH CERTAIN EXEMPT OFFERINGS.—A security is a covered security with respect to a transaction that is exempt from registration under this title pursuant to—

(A) paragraph (1) or (3) of section 4, and the issuer of such security files reports with the Commission pursuant to section 13 or 15(d) of the Securities Exchange Act of 1934;

(B) section 4(4);

(C) section 4(6)[28];

(D) a rule or regulation adopted pursuant to section 3(b)(2) and such security is—

(i) offered or sold on a national securities exchange; or

(ii) offered or sold to a qualified purchaser, as defined by the Commission pursuant to paragraph (3) with respect to that purchase or sale;

(E) section 3(a), other than the offer or sale of a security that is exempt from such registration pursuant to paragraph (4), (10), or (11) of such section, except that a

---

[28] The reference to section 4(6) in this subparagraph probably should be a reference to section 4(a)(6).

municipal security that is exempt from such registration pursuant to paragraph (2) of such section is not a covered security with respect to the offer or sale of such security in the State in which the issuer of such security is located;

(F) Commission rules or regulations issued under section 4(2), except that this subparagraph does not prohibit a State from imposing notice filing requirements that are substantially similar to those required by rule or regulation under section 4(2) that are in effect on September 1, 1996; or

(G) section 4(a)(7).

(c) PRESERVATION OF AUTHORITY.—

(1) FRAUD AUTHORITY.—Consistent with this section, the securities commission (or any agency or office performing like functions) of any State shall retain jurisdiction under the laws of such State to investigate and bring enforcement actions, in connection with securities or securities transactions [30]

(A) with respect to—
(i) fraud or deceit; or
(ii) unlawful conduct by a broker or dealer; and

(B) in connection to a transaction described under section 4(6) [31], with respect to—
(i) fraud or deceit; or
(ii) unlawful conduct by a broker, dealer, funding portal, or issuer.

(2) PRESERVATION OF FILING REQUIREMENTS.—

(A) NOTICE FILINGS PERMITTED.—Nothing in this section prohibits the securities commission (or any agency or office performing like functions) of any State from requiring the filing of any document filed with the Commission pursuant to this title, together with annual or periodic reports of the value of securities sold or offered to be sold to persons located in the State (if such sales data is not included in documents filed with the Commission), solely for notice purposes and the assessment of any fee, together with a consent to service of process and any required fee.

(B) PRESERVATION OF FEES.—

(i) IN GENERAL.—Until otherwise provided by law, rule, regulation, or order, or other administrative action of any State or any political subdivision thereof, adopted after the date of enactment of the National Securities Markets Improvement Act of 1996, filing or registration fees with respect to securities or securities transactions shall continue to be collected in amounts determined pursuant to State law as in effect on the day before such date.

(ii) SCHEDULE.—The fees required by this subparagraph shall be paid, and all necessary supporting data on sales or offers for sales required under subparagraph (A), shall be reported on the same

---

[30] In the matter preceding subparagraph (A), the word "transactions" probably should read "transactions—".

[31] The reference to section 4(6) in the matter preceding clause (i) of this subparagraph probably should be a reference to section 4(a)(6).

schedule as would have been applicable had the issuer not relied on the exemption provided in subsection (a).

(C) AVAILABILITY OF PREEMPTION CONTINGENT ON PAYMENT OF FEES.—

(i) IN GENERAL.—During the period beginning on the date of enactment of the National Securities Markets Improvement Act of 1996 and ending 3 years after that date of enactment, the securities commission (or any agency or office performing like functions) of any State may require the registration of securities issued by any issuer who refuses to pay the fees required by subparagraph (B).

(ii) DELAYS.—For purposes of this subparagraph, delays in payment of fees or underpayments of fees that are promptly remedied shall not constitute a refusal to pay fees.

(D) FEES NOT PERMITTED ON LISTED SECURITIES.—Notwithstanding subparagraphs (A), (B), and (C), no filing or fee may be required with respect to any security that is a covered security pursuant to subsection (b)(1), or will be such a covered security upon completion of the transaction, or is a security of the same issuer that is equal in seniority or that is a senior security to a security that is a covered security pursuant to subsection (b)(1).

(F)[32] FEES NOT PERMITTED ON CROWDFUNDED SECURITIES.—Notwithstanding subparagraphs (A), (B), and (C), no filing or fee may be required with respect to any security that is a covered security pursuant to subsection (b)(4)(B), or will be such a covered security upon completion of the transaction, except for the securities commission (or any agency or office performing like functions) of the State of the principal place of business of the issuer, or any State in which purchasers of 50 percent or greater of the aggregate amount of the issue are residents, provided that for purposes of this subparagraph, the term "State" includes the District of Columbia and the territories of the United States.

(3) ENFORCEMENT OF REQUIREMENTS.—Nothing in this section shall prohibit the securities commission (or any agency or office performing like functions) of any State from suspending the offer or sale of securities within such State as a result of the failure to submit any filing or fee required under law and permitted under this section.

(d) DEFINITIONS.—For purposes of this section, the following definitions shall apply:

(1) OFFERING DOCUMENT.—The term "offering document"—

(A) has the meaning given the term "prospectus" in section 2(a)(10), but without regard to the provisions of subparagraphs (a) and (b) of that section; and

(B) includes a communication that is not deemed to offer a security pursuant to a rule of the Commission.

---

[32] So in law. There is no subparagraph (E) in paragraph (2).

(2) PREPARED BY OR ON BEHALF OF THE ISSUER.—Not later than 6 months after the date of enactment of the National Securities Markets Improvement Act of 1996, the Commission shall, by rule, define the term "prepared by or on behalf of the issuer" for purposes of this section.

(3) STATE.—The term "State" has the same meaning as in section 3 of the Securities Exchange Act of 1934.

(4) SENIOR SECURITY.—The term "senior security" means any bond, debenture, note, or similar obligation or instrument constituting a security and evidencing indebtedness, and any stock of a class having priority over any other class as to distribution of assets or payment of dividends.

SPECIAL POWERS OF COMMISSION

SEC. 19. [77s] (a) The Commission shall have authority from time to time to make, amend, and rescind such rules and regulations as may be necessary to carry out the provisions of this title, including rules and regulations governing registration statements and prospectuses for various classes of securities and issuers, and defining accounting, technical and trade terms used in this title. Among other things, the Commission shall have authority, for the purposes of this title, to prescribe the form or forms in which required information shall be set forth, the items or details to be shown in the balance sheet and earning statement, and the methods to be followed in the preparation of accounts, in the appraisal or valuation of assets and liabilities, in the determination of depreciation and depletion, in the differentiation of recurring and nonrecurring income, in the differentiation of investment and operating income, and in the preparation, where the Commission deems it necessary or desirable, of consolidated balance sheets or income accounts of any person directly or indirectly controlling or controlled by the issuer, or any person under direct or indirect common control with the issuer. The rules and regulations of the Commission shall be effective upon publication in the manner which the Commission shall prescribe. No provision of this title imposing any liability shall apply to any act done or omitted in good faith in conformity with any rule or regulation of the Commission, notwithstanding that such rule or regulation may, after such act or omission, be amended or rescinded or be determined by judicial or other authority to be invalid for any reason.

(b) RECOGNITION OF ACCOUNTING STANDARDS.—

(1) IN GENERAL.—In carrying out its authority under subsection (a) and under section 13(b) of the Securities Exchange Act of 1934, the Commission may recognize, as "generally accepted" for purposes of the securities laws, any accounting principles established by a standard setting body—

(A) that—

(i) is organized as a private entity;

(ii) has, for administrative and operational purposes, a board of trustees (or equivalent body) serving in the public interest, the majority of whom are not, concurrent with their service on such board, and have not been during the 2-year period preceding such service, associated persons of any registered public accounting firm;

(iii) is funded as provided in section 109 of the Sarbanes-Oxley Act of 2002;

(iv) has adopted procedures to ensure prompt consideration, by majority vote of its members, of changes to accounting principles necessary to reflect emerging accounting issues and changing business practices; and

(v) considers, in adopting accounting principles, the need to keep standards current in order to reflect changes in the business environment, the extent to which international convergence on high quality accounting standards is necessary or appropriate in the public interest and for the protection of investors; and

(B) that the Commission determines has the capacity to assist the Commission in fulfilling the requirements of subsection (a) and section 13(b) of the Securities Exchange Act of 1934, because, at a minimum, the standard setting body is capable of improving the accuracy and effectiveness of financial reporting and the protection of investors under the securities laws.

(2) ANNUAL REPORT.—A standard setting body described in paragraph (1) shall submit an annual report to the Commission and the public, containing audited financial statements of that standard setting body.

(c) For the purpose of all investigations which, in the opinion of the Commission, are necessary and proper for the enforcement of this title, any member of the Commission or any officer or officers designated by it are empowered to administer oaths and affirmations, subpena witnesses, take evidence, and require the production of any books, papers, or other documents which the Commission deems relevant or material to the inquiry. Such attendance of witnesses and the production of such documentary evidence may be required from any place in the United States or any Territory at any designated place of hearing.

(d)(1) The Commission is authorized to cooperate with any association composed of duly constituted representatives of State governments whose primary assignment is the regulation of the securities business within those States, and which, in the judgment of the Commission, could assist in effectuating greater uniformity in Federal-State securities matters. The Commission shall, at its discretion, cooperate, coordinate, and share information with such an association for the purposes of carrying out the policies and projects set forth in paragraphs (2) and (3).

(2) It is the declared policy of this subsection that there should be greater Federal and State cooperation in securities matters, including—

(A) maximum effectiveness of regulation,

(B) maximum uniformity in Federal and State regulatory standards,

(C) minimum interference with the business of capital formation, and

Sec. 19 SECURITIES ACT OF 1933

(D) a substantial reduction in costs and paperwork to diminish the burdens of raising investment capital (particularly by small business) and to diminish the costs of the administration of the Government programs involved.

(3) The purpose of this subsection is to engender cooperation between the Commission, any such association of State securities officials, and other duly constituted securities associations in the following areas:

(A) the sharing of information regarding the registration or exemption of securities issues applied for in the various States;

(B) the development and maintenance of uniform securities forms and procedures; and

(C) the development of a uniform exemption from registration for small issuers which can be agreed upon among several States or between the States and the Federal Government. The Commission shall have the authority to adopt such an exemption as agreed upon for Federal purposes. Nothing in this Act shall be construed as authorizing preemption of State law.

(4) In order to carry out these policies and purposes, the Commission shall conduct an annual conference as well as such other meetings as are deemed necessary, to which representatives from such securities associations, securities self-regulatory organizations, agencies, and private organizations involved in capital formation shall be invited to participate.

(5) For fiscal year 1982, and for each of the three succeeding fiscal years, there are authorized to be appropriated such amounts as may be necessary and appropriate to carry out the policies, provisions, and purposes of this subsection. Any sums so appropriated shall remain available until expended.

(6) Notwithstanding any other provision of law, neither the Commission nor any other person shall be required to establish any procedures not specifically required by the securities laws, as that term is defined in section 3(a)(47) of the Securities Exchange Act of 1934, or by chapter 5 of title 5, United States Code, in connection with cooperation, coordination, or consultation with—

(A) any association referred to in paragraph (1) or (3) or any conference or meeting referred to in paragraph (4), while such association, conference, or meeting is carrying out activities in furtherance of the provisions of this subsection; or

(B) any forum, agency or organization, or group referred to in section 503 of the Small Business Investment Incentive Act of 1980, while such forum, agency, organization, or group is carrying out activities in furtherance of the provisions of such section 503.

As used in this paragraph, the terms "association", "conference", "meeting", "forum", "agency", "organization", and "group" include any committee, subgroup, or representative of such entities.

(e) EVALUATION OF RULES OR PROGRAMS.—For the purpose of evaluating any rule or program of the Commission issued or carried out under any provision of the securities laws, as defined in section 3 of the Securities Exchange Act of 1934 (15 U.S.C. 78c), and the purposes of considering, proposing, adopting, or engaging in any such rule or program or developing new rules or programs, the Commission may—

(1) gather information from and communicate with investors or other members of the public;

(2) engage in such temporary investor testing programs as the Commission determines are in the public interest or would protect investors; and

(3) consult with academics and consultants, as necessary to carry out this subsection.

(f) RULE OF CONSTRUCTION.—For purposes of the Paperwork Reduction Act (44 U.S.C. 3501 et seq.), any action taken under subsection (e) shall not be construed to be a collection of information.

(g) FUNDING FOR THE GASB.—

(1) IN GENERAL.—The Commission may, subject to the limitations imposed by section 15B of the Securities Exchange Act of 1934 (15 U.S.C. 78o–4), require a national securities association registered under the Securities Exchange Act of 1934 to establish—

(A) a reasonable annual accounting support fee to adequately fund the annual budget of the Governmental Accounting Standards Board (referred to in this subsection as the "GASB"); and

(B) rules and procedures, in consultation with the principal organizations representing State governors, legislators, local elected officials, and State and local finance officers, to provide for the equitable allocation, assessment, and collection of the accounting support fee established under subparagraph (A) from the members of the association, and the remittance of all such accounting support fees to the Financial Accounting Foundation.

(2) ANNUAL BUDGET.—For purposes of this subsection, the annual budget of the GASB is the annual budget reviewed and approved according to the internal procedures of the Financial Accounting Foundation.

(3) USE OF FUNDS.—Any fees or funds collected under this subsection shall be used to support the efforts of the GASB to establish standards of financial accounting and reporting recognized as generally accepted accounting principles applicable to State and local governments of the United States.

(4) LIMITATION ON FEE.—The annual accounting support fees collected under this subsection for a fiscal year shall not exceed the recoverable annual budgeted expenses of the GASB (which may include operating expenses, capital, and accrued items).

(5) RULES OF CONSTRUCTION.—

(A) FEES NOT PUBLIC MONIES.—Accounting support fees collected under this subsection and other receipts of the GASB shall not be considered public monies of the United States.

(B) LIMITATION ON AUTHORITY OF THE COMMISSION.—Nothing in this subsection shall be construed to—

(i) provide the Commission or any national securities association direct or indirect oversight of the budget or technical agenda of the GASB; or

(ii) affect the setting of generally accepted accounting principles by the GASB.

(C) NONINTERFERENCE WITH STATES.—Nothing in this subsection shall be construed to impair or limit the authority of a State or local government to establish accounting and financial reporting standards.

INJUNCTIONS AND PROSECUTION OF OFFENSES

SEC. 20. [77t] (a) Whenever it shall appear to the Commission, either upon complaint or otherwise, that the provisions of this title, or of any rule or regulation prescribed under authority thereof, have been or are about to be violated, it may, in its discretion, either require or permit such person to file with it a statement in writing, under oath, or otherwise, as to all the facts and circumstances concerning the subject matter which it believes to be in the public interest to investigate, and may investigate such facts.

(b) Whenever it shall appear to the Commission that any person is engaged or about to engage in any acts or practices which constitute or will constitute a violation of the provisions of this title, or of any rule or regulation prescribed under authority thereof, the Commission may, in its discretion, bring an action in any district court of the United States, or United States court of any Territory, to enjoin such acts or practices, and upon a proper showing, a permanent or temporary injunction or restraining order shall be granted without bond. The Commission may transmit such evidence as may be available concerning such acts or practices to the Attorney General who may, in his discretion, institute the necessary criminal proceedings under this title. Any such criminal proceeding may be brought either in the district wherein the transmittal of the prospectus or security complained of begins, or in the district wherein such prospectus or security is received.

(c) Upon application of the Commission, the district courts of the United States and the United States courts of any Territory shall have jurisdiction to issue writs of mandamus commanding any person to comply with the provisions of this title or any order of the Commission made in pursuance thereof.

(d) MONEY PENALTIES IN CIVIL ACTIONS.—

(1) AUTHORITY OF COMMISSION.—Whenever it shall appear to the Commission that any person has violated any provision of this title, the rules or regulations thereunder, or a cease-and-desist order entered by the Commission pursuant to section 8A of this title, other than by committing a violation subject to a penalty pursuant to section 21A of the Securities Exchange Act of 1934, the Commission may bring an action in a United States district court to seek, and the court shall have jurisdiction to impose, upon a proper showing, a civil penalty to be paid by the person who committed such violation.

(2) AMOUNT OF PENALTY.—

(A) FIRST TIER.—The amount of the penalty shall be determined by the court in light of the facts and circumstances. For each violation, the amount of the penalty shall not exceed the greater of (i) $5,000 for a natural person or $50,000 for any other person, or (ii) the gross amount of pecuniary gain to such defendant as a result of the violation.

(B) SECOND TIER.—Notwithstanding subparagraph (A), the amount of penalty for each such violation shall not exceed the greater of (i) $50,000 for a natural person or $250,000 for any other person, or (ii) the gross amount of pecuniary gain to such defendant as a result of the violation, if the violation described in paragraph (1) involved fraud, deceit, manipulation, or deliberate or reckless disregard of a regulatory requirement.

(C) THIRD TIER.—Notwithstanding subparagraphs (A) and (B), the amount of penalty for each such violation shall not exceed the greater of (i) $100,000 for a natural person or $500,000 for any other person, or (ii) the gross amount of pecuniary gain to such defendant as a result of the violation, if—

(I)[33] the violation described in paragraph (1) involved fraud, deceit, manipulation, or deliberate or reckless disregard of a regulatory requirement; and

(II)[33] such violation directly or indirectly resulted in substantial losses or created a significant risk of substantial losses to other persons.

(3) PROCEDURES FOR COLLECTION.—

(A) PAYMENT OF PENALTY TO TREASURY.—A penalty imposed under this section shall be payable into the Treasury of the United States, except as otherwise provided in section 308 of the Sarbanes-Oxley Act of 2002 and section 21F of the Securities Exchange Act of 1934.

(B) COLLECTION OF PENALTIES.—If a person upon whom such a penalty is imposed shall fail to pay such penalty within the time prescribed in the court's order, the Commission may refer the matter to the Attorney General who shall recover such penalty by action in the appropriate United States district court.

(C) REMEDY NOT EXCLUSIVE.—The actions authorized by this subsection may be brought in addition to any other action that the Commission or the Attorney General is entitled to bring.

(D) JURISDICTION AND VENUE.—For purposes of section 22 of this title, actions under this section shall be actions to enforce a liability or a duty created by this title.

(4) SPECIAL PROVISIONS RELATING TO A VIOLATION OF A CEASE-AND-DESIST ORDER.—In an action to enforce a cease-and-desist order entered by the Commission pursuant to section 8A, each separate violation of such order shall be a separate offense, except that in the case of a violation through a continuing failure to comply with such an order, each day of the failure to comply with the order shall be deemed a separate offense.

(e) AUTHORITY OF A COURT TO PROHIBIT PERSONS FROM SERVING AS OFFICERS AND DIRECTORS.—In any proceeding under sub-

---

[33] So in law. Probably should be clauses (i) and (ii).

section (b), the court may prohibit, conditionally or unconditionally, and permanently or for such period of time as it shall determine, any person who violated section 17(a)(1) of this title from acting as an officer or director of any issuer that has a class of securities registered pursuant to section 12 of the Securities Exchange Act of 1934 or that is required to file reports pursuant to section 15(d) of such Act if the person's conduct demonstrates unfitness to serve as an officer or director of any such issuer.

(f) PROHIBITION OF ATTORNEYS' FEES PAID FROM COMMISSION DISGORGEMENT FUNDS.—Except as otherwise ordered by the court upon motion by the Commission, or, in the case of an administrative action, as otherwise ordered by the Commission, funds disgorged as the result of an action brought by the Commission in Federal court, or as a result of any Commission administrative action, shall not be distributed as payment for attorneys' fees or expenses incurred by private parties seeking distribution of the disgorged funds.

(g) AUTHORITY OF A COURT TO PROHIBIT PERSONS FROM PARTICIPATING IN AN OFFERING OF PENNY STOCK.—

(1) IN GENERAL.—In any proceeding under subsection (a) against any person participating in, or, at the time of the alleged misconduct, who was participating in, an offering of penny stock, the court may prohibit that person from participating in an offering of penny stock, conditionally or unconditionally, and permanently or for such period of time as the court shall determine.

(2) DEFINITION.—For purposes of this subsection, the term "person participating in an offering of penny stock" includes any person engaging in activities with a broker, dealer, or issuer for purposes of issuing, trading, or inducing or attempting to induce the purchase or sale of, any penny stock. The Commission may, by rule or regulation, define such term to include other activities, and may, by rule, regulation, or order, exempt any person or class of persons, in whole or in part, conditionally or unconditionally, from inclusion in such term.

HEARINGS BY COMMISSION

SEC. 21. [77u] All hearings shall be public and may be held before the Commission or an officer or officers of the Commission designated by it, and appropriate records thereof shall be kept.

JURISDICTION OF OFFENSES AND SUITS

SEC. 22. [77v] (a) The district courts of the United States and United States courts of any Territory shall have jurisdiction of offenses and violations under this title and under the rules and regulations promulgated by the Commission in respect thereto, and, concurrent with State and Territorial courts, except as provided in section 16 with respect to covered class actions, of all suits in equity and actions at law brought to enforce any liability or duty created by this title. Any such suit or action may be brought in the district wherein the defendant is found or is an inhabitant or transacts business, or in the district where the offer or sale took place, if the defendant participated therein, and process in such cases may be served in any other district of which the defendant is an inhabitant or wherever the defendant may be found. In any action or proceeding instituted by the Commission under this title in a United States district court for any judicial district, a subpoena issued to compel the attendance of a witness or the production of documents or tangible things (or both) at a hearing or trial may be served at any place within the United States. Rule 45(c)(3)(A)(ii) of the Federal Rules of Civil Procedure shall not apply to a subpoena issued under the preceding sentence. Judgments and decrees so rendered shall be subject to review as provided in sections 1254, 1291, 1292, and 1294 of title 28, United States Code. Except as provided in section 16(c), no case arising under this title and brought in any State court of competent jurisdiction shall be removed to any court of the United States. No costs shall be assessed for or against the Commission in any proceeding under this title brought by or against it in the Supreme Court or such other courts.

(b) In case of contumacy or refusal to obey a subpena issued to any person, any of the said United States courts, within the jurisdiction of which said person guilty of contumacy or refusal to obey is found or resides, upon application by the Commission may issue to such person an order requiring such person to appear before the Commission, or one of its examiners designated by it, there to produce documentary evidence if so ordered, or there to give evidence touching the matter in question; and any failure to obey such order of the court may be punished by said court as a contempt thereof.[34]

(c) EXTRATERRITORIAL JURISDICTION.—The district courts of the United States and the United States courts of any Territory shall have jurisdiction of an action or proceeding brought or instituted by the Commission or the United States alleging a violation of section 17(a) involving—

(1) conduct within the United States that constitutes significant steps in furtherance of the violation, even if the securities transaction occurs outside the United States and involves only foreign investors; or

(2) conduct occurring outside the United States that has a foreseeable substantial effect within the United States.

UNLAWFUL REPRESENTATIONS

SEC. 23. [77w] Neither the fact that the registration statement for a security has been filed or is in effect nor the fact that a stop order is not in effect with respect thereto shall be deemed a finding by the Commission that registration statement is true and accurate on its face or that it does not contain an untrue statement of fact or omit to state a material fact, or be held to mean that the Commission has in any way passed upon the merits of, or given approval to, such security. It shall be unlawful to make, or

---

[34] Subsection (c) of section 22, which related to the immunity from prosecution of an individual compelled to testify or produce evidence, after claiming his privilege against self-incrimination, was repealed by the Organized Crime Control Act of 1970 (Pub. L. 91–542, 84 Stat. 929), which made applicable in lieu thereof 18 U.S.C. 6001, 6002, 6004. [Printed in appendix to this volume.]

cause to be made, to any prospective purchaser any representation contrary to the foregoing provisions of this section.

PENALTIES

SEC. 24. [77x] Any person who willfully violates any of the provisions of this title, or the rules and regulations promulgated by the Commission under authority thereof, or any person who willfully, in a registration statement filed under this title, makes any untrue statement of a material fact or omits to state any material fact required to be stated therein or necessary to make the statements therein not misleading, shall upon conviction be fined not more than $10,000 or imprisoned not more than five years, or both.[35]

JURISDICTION OF OTHER GOVERNMENT AGENCIES OVER SECURITIES

SEC. 25. [77y] Nothing in this title shall relieve any person from submitting to the respective supervisory units of the Government of the United States information, reports, or other documents that are now or may hereafter be required by any provision of law.

SEPARABILITY OF PROVISIONS

SEC. 26. [77z] If any provision of this Act, or the application of such provision to any person or circumstance, shall be held invalid, the remainder of this Act, or the application of such provision to persons or circumstances other than those as to which it is held invalid, shall not be affected thereby.

SEC. 27. [77z-1] PRIVATE SECURITIES LITIGATION.

(a) PRIVATE CLASS ACTIONS.—

(1) IN GENERAL.—The provisions of this subsection shall apply to each private action arising under this title that is brought as a plaintiff class action pursuant to the Federal Rules of Civil Procedure.

(2) CERTIFICATION FILED WITH COMPLAINT.—

(A) IN GENERAL.—Each plaintiff seeking to serve as a representative party on behalf of a class shall provide a sworn certification, which shall be personally signed by such plaintiff and filed with the complaint, that—

(i) states that the plaintiff has reviewed the complaint and authorized its filing;

(ii) states that the plaintiff did not purchase the security that is the subject of the complaint at the direction of plaintiff's counsel or in order to participate in any private action arising under this title;

(iii) states that the plaintiff is willing to serve as a representative party on behalf of a class, including providing testimony at deposition and trial, if necessary;

(iv) sets forth all of the transactions of the plaintiff in the security that is the subject of the complaint during the class period specified in the complaint;

---

[35] See also 18 U.S.C. 3623. [Printed in appendix to this volume.]

(v) identifies any other action under this title, filed during the 3-year period preceding the date on which the certification is signed by the plaintiff, in which the plaintiff has sought to serve, or served, as a representative party on behalf of a class; and

(vi) states that the plaintiff will not accept any payment for serving as a representative party on behalf of a class beyond the plaintiff's pro rata share of any recovery, except as ordered or approved by the court in accordance with paragraph (4).

(B) NONWAIVER OF ATTORNEY-CLIENT PRIVILEGE.—The certification filed pursuant to subparagraph (A) shall not be construed to be a waiver of the attorney-client privilege.

(3) APPOINTMENT OF LEAD PLAINTIFF.—

(A) EARLY NOTICE TO CLASS MEMBERS.—

(i) IN GENERAL.—Not later than 20 days after the date on which the complaint is filed, the plaintiff or plaintiffs shall cause to be published, in a widely circulated national business-oriented publication or wire service, a notice advising members of the purported plaintiff class—

(I) of the pendency of the action, the claims asserted therein, and the purported class period; and

(II) that, not later than 60 days after the date on which the notice is published, any member of the purported class may move the court to serve as lead plaintiff of the purported class.

(ii) MULTIPLE ACTIONS.—If more than one action on behalf of a class asserting substantially the same claim or claims arising under this title is filed, only the plaintiff or plaintiffs in the first filed action shall be required to cause notice to be published in accordance with clause (i).

(iii) ADDITIONAL NOTICES MAY BE REQUIRED UNDER FEDERAL RULES.—Notice required under clause (i) shall be in addition to any notice required pursuant to the Federal Rules of Civil Procedure.

(B) APPOINTMENT OF LEAD PLAINTIFF.—

(i) IN GENERAL.—Not later than 90 days after the date on which a notice is published under subparagraph (A)(i), the court shall consider any motion made by a purported class member in response to the notice, including any motion by a class member who is not individually named as a plaintiff in the complaint or complaints, and shall appoint as lead plaintiff the member or members of the purported plaintiff class that the court determines to be most capable of adequately representing the interests of class members (hereafter in this paragraph referred to as the "most adequate plaintiff") in accordance with this subparagraph.

(ii) CONSOLIDATED ACTIONS.—If more than one action on behalf of a class asserting substantially the same claim or claims arising under this title has been filed, and any party has sought to consolidate those actions for pretrial purposes or for trial, the court shall not make the determination required by clause (i) until after the decision on the motion to consolidate is rendered. As soon as practicable after such decision is rendered, the court shall appoint the most adequate plaintiff as lead plaintiff for the consolidated actions in accordance with this subparagraph.

(iii) REBUTTABLE PRESUMPTION.—

(I) IN GENERAL.—Subject to subclause (II), for purposes of clause (i), the court shall adopt a presumption that the most adequate plaintiff in any private action arising under this title is the person or group of persons that—

(aa) has either filed the complaint or made a motion in response to a notice under subparagraph (A)(i);

(bb) in the determination of the court, has the largest financial interest in the relief sought by the class; and

(cc) otherwise satisfies the requirements of Rule 23 of the Federal Rules of Civil Procedure.

(II) REBUTTAL EVIDENCE.—The presumption described in subclause (I) may be rebutted only upon proof by a member of the purported plaintiff class that the presumptively most adequate plaintiff—

(aa) will not fairly and adequately protect the interests of the class; or

(bb) is subject to unique defenses that render such plaintiff incapable of adequately representing the class.

(iv) DISCOVERY.—For purposes of this subparagraph, discovery relating to whether a member or members of the purported plaintiff class is the most adequate plaintiff may be conducted by a plaintiff only if the plaintiff first demonstrates a reasonable basis for a finding that the presumptively most adequate plaintiff is incapable of adequately representing the class.

(v) SELECTION OF LEAD COUNSEL.—The most adequate plaintiff shall, subject to the approval of the court, select and retain counsel to represent the class.

(vi) RESTRICTIONS ON PROFESSIONAL PLAINTIFFS.— Except as the court may otherwise permit, consistent with the purposes of this section, a person may be a lead plaintiff, or an officer, director, or fiduciary of a lead plaintiff, in no more than 5 securities class actions brought as plaintiff class actions pursuant to the Federal Rules of Civil Procedure during any 3-year period.

(4) RECOVERY BY PLAINTIFFS.—The share of any final judgment or of any settlement that is awarded to a representative party serving on behalf of a class shall be equal, on a per share basis, to the portion of the final judgment or settlement awarded to all other members of the class. Nothing in this paragraph shall be construed to limit the award of reasonable costs and expenses (including lost wages) directly relating to the representation of the class to any representative party serving on behalf of the class.

(5) RESTRICTIONS ON SETTLEMENTS UNDER SEAL.—The terms and provisions of any settlement agreement of a class action shall not be filed under seal, except that on motion of any party to the settlement, the court may order filing under seal for those portions of a settlement agreement as to which good cause is shown for such filing under seal. For purposes of this paragraph, good cause shall exist only if publication of a term or provision of a settlement agreement would cause direct and substantial harm to any party.

(6) RESTRICTIONS ON PAYMENT OF ATTORNEYS' FEES AND EXPENSES.—Total attorneys' fees and expenses awarded by the court to counsel for the plaintiff class shall not exceed a reasonable percentage of the amount of any damages and prejudgment interest actually paid to the class.

(7) DISCLOSURE OF SETTLEMENT TERMS TO CLASS MEMBERS.—Any proposed or final settlement agreement that is published or otherwise disseminated to the class shall include each of the following statements, along with a cover page summarizing the information contained in such statements:

(A) STATEMENT OF PLAINTIFF RECOVERY.—The amount of the settlement proposed to be distributed to the parties to the action, determined in the aggregate and on an average per share basis.

(B) STATEMENT OF POTENTIAL OUTCOME OF CASE.—

(i) AGREEMENT ON AMOUNT OF DAMAGES.—If the settling parties agree on the average amount of damages per share that would be recoverable if the plaintiff prevailed on each claim alleged under this title, a statement concerning the average amount of such potential damages per share.

(ii) DISAGREEMENT ON AMOUNT OF DAMAGES.—If the parties do not agree on the average amount of damages per share that would be recoverable if the plaintiff prevailed on each claim alleged under this title, a statement from each settling party concerning the issue or issues on which the parties disagree.

(iii) INADMISSIBILITY FOR CERTAIN PURPOSES.—A statement made in accordance with clause (i) or (ii) concerning the amount of damages shall not be admissible in any Federal or State judicial action or administrative proceeding, other than an action or proceeding arising out of such statement.

(C) STATEMENT OF ATTORNEYS' FEES OR COSTS SOUGHT.—If any of the settling parties or their counsel intend to apply to the court for an award of attorneys' fees or costs from any fund established as part of the settlement, a statement indicating which parties or counsel intend to make such an application, the amount of fees and costs that will be sought (including the amount of such fees and costs determined on an average per share basis), and a brief explanation supporting the fees and costs sought.

(D) IDENTIFICATION OF LAWYERS' REPRESENTATIVES.—The name, telephone number, and address of one or more representatives of counsel for the plaintiff class who will be reasonably available to answer questions from class members concerning any matter contained in any notice of settlement published or otherwise disseminated to the class.

(E) REASONS FOR SETTLEMENT.—A brief statement explaining the reasons why the parties are proposing the settlement.

(F) OTHER INFORMATION.—Such other information as may be required by the court.

(8) ATTORNEY CONFLICT OF INTEREST.—If a plaintiff class is represented by an attorney who directly owns or otherwise has a beneficial interest in the securities that are the subject of the litigation, the court shall make a determination of whether such ownership or other interest constitutes a conflict of interest sufficient to disqualify the attorney from representing the plaintiff class.

(b) STAY OF DISCOVERY; PRESERVATION OF EVIDENCE.—

(1) IN GENERAL.—In any private action arising under this title, all discovery and other proceedings shall be stayed during the pendency of any motion to dismiss, unless the court finds, upon the motion of any party, that particularized discovery is necessary to preserve evidence or to prevent undue prejudice to that party.

(2) PRESERVATION OF EVIDENCE.—During the pendency of any stay of discovery pursuant to this subsection, unless otherwise ordered by the court, any party to the action with actual notice of the allegations contained in the complaint shall treat all documents, data compilations (including electronically recorded or stored data), and tangible objects that are in the custody or control of such person and that are relevant to the allegations, as if they were the subject of a continuing request for production of documents from an opposing party under the Federal Rules of Civil Procedure.

(3) SANCTION FOR WILLFUL VIOLATION.—A party aggrieved by the willful failure of an opposing party to comply with paragraph (2) may apply to the court for an order awarding appropriate sanctions.

(4) CIRCUMVENTION OF STAY OF DISCOVERY.—Upon a proper showing, a court may stay discovery proceedings in any private action in a State court as necessary in aid of its jurisdiction, or to protect or effectuate its judgments, in an action subject to a stay of discovery pursuant to this subsection.

(c) SANCTIONS FOR ABUSIVE LITIGATION.—

(1) MANDATORY REVIEW BY COURT.—In any private action arising under this title, upon final adjudication of the action, the court shall include in the record specific findings regarding compliance by each party and each attorney representing any party with each requirement of Rule 11(b) of the Federal Rules of Civil Procedure as to any complaint, responsive pleading, or dispositive motion.

(2) MANDATORY SANCTIONS.—If the court makes a finding under paragraph (1) that a party or attorney violated any requirement of Rule 11(b) of the Federal Rules of Civil Procedure as to any complaint, responsive pleading, or dispositive motion, the court shall impose sanctions on such party or attorney in accordance with Rule 11 of the Federal Rules of Civil Procedure. Prior to making a finding that any party or attorney has violated Rule 11 of the Federal Rules of Civil Procedure, the court shall give such party or attorney notice and an opportunity to respond.

(3) PRESUMPTION IN FAVOR OF ATTORNEYS' FEES AND COSTS.—

(A) IN GENERAL.—Subject to subparagraphs (B) and (C), for purposes of paragraph (2), the court shall adopt a presumption that the appropriate sanction—

(i) for failure of any responsive pleading or dispositive motion to comply with any requirement of Rule 11(b) of the Federal Rules of Civil Procedure is an award to the opposing party of the reasonable attorneys' fees and other expenses incurred as a direct result of the violation; and

(ii) for substantial failure of any complaint to comply with any requirement of Rule 11(b) of the Federal Rules of Civil Procedure is an award to the opposing party of the reasonable attorneys' fees and other expenses incurred in the action.

(B) REBUTTAL EVIDENCE.—The presumption described in subparagraph (A) may be rebutted only upon proof by the party or attorney against whom sanctions are to be imposed that—

(i) the award of attorneys' fees and other expenses will impose an unreasonable burden on that party or attorney and would be unjust, and the failure to make such an award would not impose a greater burden on the party in whose favor sanctions are to be imposed; or

(ii) the violation of Rule 11(b) of the Federal Rules of Civil Procedure was de minimis.

(C) SANCTIONS.—If the party or attorney against whom sanctions are to be imposed meets its burden under subparagraph (B), the court shall award the sanctions that the court deems appropriate pursuant to Rule 11 of the Federal Rules of Civil Procedure.

(d) DEFENDANT'S RIGHT TO WRITTEN INTERROGATORIES.—In any private action arising under this title in which the plaintiff may recover money damages only on proof that a defendant acted with a particular state of mind, the court shall, when requested by a defendant, submit to the jury a written interrogatory on the issue of each such defendant's state of mind at the time the alleged violation occurred.

SEC. 27A. [77z-2] APPLICATION OF SAFE HARBOR FOR FORWARD-LOOKING STATEMENTS.

(a) APPLICABILITY.—This section shall apply only to a forward-looking statement made by—

(1) an issuer that, at the time that the statement is made, is subject to the reporting requirements of section 13(a) or section 15(d) of the Securities Exchange Act of 1934;

(2) a person acting on behalf of such issuer;

(3) an outside reviewer retained by such issuer making a statement on behalf of such issuer; or

(4) an underwriter, with respect to information provided by such issuer or information derived from information provided by the issuer.

(b) EXCLUSIONS.—Except to the extent otherwise specifically provided by rule, regulation, or order of the Commission, this section shall not apply to a forward-looking statement—

(1) that is made with respect to the business or operations of the issuer, if the issuer—

(A) during the 3-year period preceding the date on which the statement was first made—

(i) was convicted of any felony or misdemeanor described in clauses (i) through (iv) of section 15(b)(4)(B) of the Securities Exchange Act of 1934; or

(ii) has been made the subject of a judicial or administrative decree or order arising out of a governmental action that—

(I) prohibits future violations of the antifraud provisions of the securities laws;

(II) requires that the issuer cease and desist from violating the antifraud provisions of the securities laws; or

(III) determines that the issuer violated the antifraud provisions of the securities laws;

(B) makes the forward-looking statement in connection with an offering of securities by a blank check company;

(C) issues penny stock;

(D) makes the forward-looking statement in connection with a rollup transaction; or

(E) makes the forward-looking statement in connection with a going private transaction; or

(2) that is—

(A) included in a financial statement prepared in accordance with generally accepted accounting principles;

(B) contained in a registration statement of, or otherwise issued by, an investment company;

(C) made in connection with a tender offer;

(D) made in connection with an initial public offering;

(E) made in connection with an offering by, or relating to the operations of, a partnership, limited liability company, or a direct participation investment program; or

(F) made in a disclosure of beneficial ownership in a report required to be filed with the Commission pursuant to section 13(d) of the Securities Exchange Act of 1934.

(c) SAFE HARBOR.—

(1) IN GENERAL.—Except as provided in subsection (b), in any private action arising under this title that is based on an untrue statement of a material fact or omission of a material fact necessary to make the statement not misleading, a person referred to in subsection (a) shall not be liable with respect to any forward-looking statement, whether written or oral, if and to the extent that—

(A) the forward-looking statement is—

(i) identified as a forward-looking statement, and is accompanied by meaningful cautionary statements identifying important factors that could cause actual results to differ materially from those in the forward-looking statement; or

(ii) immaterial; or

(B) the plaintiff fails to prove that the forward-looking statement—

(i) if made by a natural person, was made with actual knowledge by that person that the statement was false or misleading; or

(ii) if made by a business entity, was—

(I) made by or with the approval of an executive officer of that entity, and

(II) made or approved by such officer with actual knowledge by that officer that the statement was false or misleading.

(2) ORAL FORWARD-LOOKING STATEMENTS.—In the case of an oral forward-looking statement made by an issuer that is subject to the reporting requirements of section 13(a) or section 15(d) of the Securities Exchange Act of 1934, or by a person acting on behalf of such issuer, the requirement set forth in paragraph (1)(A) shall be deemed to be satisfied—

(A) if the oral forward-looking statement is accompanied by a cautionary statement—

(i) that the particular oral statement is a forward-looking statement; and

(ii) that the actual results could differ materially from those projected in the forward-looking statement; and

(B) if—

(i) the oral forward-looking statement is accompanied by an oral statement that additional information concerning factors that could cause actual results to differ materially from those in the forward-looking statement is contained in a readily available written document, or portion thereof;

(ii) the accompanying oral statement referred to in clause (i) identifies the document, or portion thereof, that contains the additional information about those factors relating to the forward-looking statement; and

(iii) the information contained in that written document is a cautionary statement that satisfies the standard established in paragraph (1)(A).

(3) AVAILABILITY.—Any document filed with the Commission or generally disseminated shall be deemed to be readily available for purposes of paragraph (2).

(4) EFFECT ON OTHER SAFE HARBORS.—The exemption provided for in paragraph (1) shall be in addition to any exemption that the Commission may establish by rule or regulation under subsection (g).

(d) DUTY TO UPDATE.—Nothing in this section shall impose upon any person a duty to update a forward-looking statement.

(e) DISPOSITIVE MOTION.—On any motion to dismiss based upon subsection (c)(1), the court shall consider any statement cited in the complaint and cautionary statement accompanying the forward-looking statement, which are not subject to material dispute, cited by the defendant.

(f) STAY PENDING DECISION ON MOTION.—In any private action arising under this title, the court shall stay discovery (other than discovery that is specifically directed to the applicability of the exemption provided for in this section) during the pendency of any motion by a defendant for summary judgment that is based on the grounds that—

(1) the statement or omission upon which the complaint is based is a forward-looking statement within the meaning of this section; and

(2) the exemption provided for in this section precludes a claim for relief.

(g) EXEMPTION AUTHORITY.—In addition to the exemptions provided for in this section, the Commission may, by rule or regulation, provide exemptions from or under any provision of this title, including with respect to liability that is based on a statement or that is based on projections or other forward-looking information, if and to the extent that any such exemption is consistent with the public interest and the protection of investors, as determined by the Commission.

(h) EFFECT ON OTHER AUTHORITY OF COMMISSION.—Nothing in this section limits, either expressly or by implication, the authority of the Commission to exercise similar authority or to adopt similar rules and regulations with respect to forward-looking statements under any other statute under which the Commission exercises rulemaking authority.

(i) DEFINITIONS.—For purposes of this section, the following definitions shall apply:

(1) FORWARD-LOOKING STATEMENT.—The term "forward-looking statement" means—

(A) a statement containing a projection of revenues, income (including income loss), earnings (including earnings loss) per share, capital expenditures, dividends, capital structure, or other financial items;

(B) a statement of the plans and objectives of management for future operations, including plans or objectives relating to the products or services of the issuer;

(C) a statement of future economic performance, including any such statement contained in a discussion and analysis of financial condition by the management or in the results of operations included pursuant to the rules and regulations of the Commission;

(D) any statement of the assumptions underlying or relating to any statement described in subparagraph (A), (B), or (C);

(E) any report issued by an outside reviewer retained by an issuer, to the extent that the report assesses a forward-looking statement made by the issuer; or

(F) a statement containing a projection or estimate of such other items as may be specified by rule or regulation of the Commission.

(2) INVESTMENT COMPANY.—The term "investment company" has the same meaning as in section 3(a) of the Investment Company Act of 1940.

(3) PENNY STOCK.—The term "penny stock" has the same meaning as in section 3(a)(51) of the Securities Exchange Act of 1934, and the rules and regulations, or orders issued pursuant to that section.

(4) GOING PRIVATE TRANSACTION.—The term "going private transaction" has the meaning given that term under the rules or regulations of the Commission issued pursuant to section 13(e) of the Securities Exchange Act of 1934.

(5) SECURITIES LAWS.—The term "securities laws" has the same meaning as in section 3 of the Securities Exchange Act of 1934.

(6) PERSON ACTING ON BEHALF OF AN ISSUER.—The term "person acting on behalf of an issuer" means an officer, director, or employee of the issuer.

(7) OTHER TERMS.—The terms "blank check company", "rollup transaction", "partnership", "limited liability company", "executive officer of an entity" and "direct participation investment program", have the meanings given those terms by rule or regulation of the Commission.

SEC. 27B. [15 U.S.C. 77z–2a] CONFLICTS OF INTEREST RELATING TO CERTAIN SECURITIZATIONS.

(a) IN GENERAL.—An underwriter, placement agent, initial purchaser, or sponsor, or any affiliate or subsidiary of any such entity, of an asset-backed security (as such term is defined in section 3 of the Securities and Exchange Act of 1934 (15 U.S.C. 78c), which for the purposes of this section shall include a synthetic asset-backed security), shall not, at any time for a period ending on the date that is one year after the date of the first closing of the sale of the asset-backed security, engage in any transaction that would involve or result in any material conflict of interest with respect to any investor in a transaction arising out of such activity.

(b) RULEMAKING.—Not later than 270 days after the date of enactment of this section, the Commission shall issue rules for the purpose of implementing subsection (a).

(c) EXCEPTION.—The prohibitions of subsection (a) shall not apply to—

(1) risk-mitigating hedging activities in connection with positions or holdings arising out of the underwriting, placement, initial purchase, or sponsorship of an asset-backed security, provided that such activities are designed to reduce the specific risks to the underwriter, placement agent, initial purchaser, or sponsor associated with positions or holdings arising out of such underwriting, placement, initial purchase, or sponsorship; or

(2) purchases or sales of asset-backed securities made pursuant to and consistent with—

(A) commitments of the underwriter, placement agent, initial purchaser, or sponsor, or any affiliate or subsidiary of any such entity, to provide liquidity for the asset-backed security, or

(B) bona fide market-making in the asset backed security.

(d) RULE OF CONSTRUCTION.—This subsection shall not otherwise limit the application of section 15G of the Securities Exchange Act of 1934.

SEC. 28. [77z-3] GENERAL EXEMPTIVE AUTHORITY.

The Commission, by rule or regulation, may conditionally or unconditionally exempt any person, security, or transaction, or any class or classes of persons, securities, or transactions, from any provision or provisions of this title or of any rule or regulation issued under this title, to the extent that such exemption is necessary or appropriate in the public interest, and is consistent with the protection of investors.

SCHEDULE A [77AA] (1) THE NAME UNDER WHICH THE ISSUER IS DOING OR INTENDS TO DO BUSINESS;

(2) the name of the State or other sovereign power under which the issuer is organized;

(3) the location of the issuer's principal business office, and if the issuer is a foreign or territorial person, the name and address of its agent in the United States authorized to receive notice;

(4) the names and addresses of the directors or persons performing similar functions, and the chief executive, financial and accounting officers, chosen or to be chosen if the issuer be a corporation, association, trust, or other entity; of all partners, if the issuer be a partnership; and of the issuer, if the issuer be an individual; and of the promoters in the case of a business to be formed, or formed within two years prior to the filing of the registration statement;

(5) the names and addresses of the underwriters;

(6) the names and addresses of all persons, if any, owning of record or beneficially, if known, more than 10 per centum of any class of stock of the issuer, or more than 10 per centum in the aggregate of the outstanding stock of the issuer as of a date within twenty days prior to the filing of the registration statement;

(7) the amount of securities of the issuer held by any person specified in paragraphs (4), (5), and (6) of this schedule, as of a date within twenty days prior to the filing of the registration statement, and, if possible, as of one year prior thereto, and the amount

of the securities, for which the registration statement is filed, to which such persons have indicated their intention to subscribe;

(8) the general character of the business actually transacted or to be transacted by the issuer;

(9) a statement of the capitalization of the issuer, including the authorized and outstanding amounts of its capital stock and the proportion thereof paid up, the number and classes of shares in which such capital stock is divided, par value thereof, or if it has no par value, the stated or assigned value thereof, a description of the respective voting rights, preferences, conversion and exchange rights, rights to dividends, profits, or capital of each class, with respect to each other class, including the retirement and liquidation rights or values thereof;

(10) a statement of the securities, if any, covered by options outstanding or to be created in connection with the security to be offered, together with the names and addresses of all persons, if any, to be allotted more than 10 per centum in the aggregate of such options;

(11) the amount of capital stock of each class issued or included in the shares of stock to be offered;

(12) the amount of the funded debt outstanding and to be created by the security to be offered, with a brief description of the date, maturity, and character of such debt, rate of interest, character of amortization provisions, and the security, if any, therefor. If substitution of any security is permissible, a summarized statement of the conditions under which such substitution is permitted. If substitution is permissible without notice, a specific statement to that effect;

(13) the specific purposes in detail and the approximate amounts to be devoted to such purposes, so far as determinable, for which the security to be offered is to supply funds, and if the funds are to be raised in part from other sources, the amounts thereof and the sources thereof, shall be stated;

(14) the remuneration, paid or estimated to be paid, by the issuer or its predecessor, directly or indirectly, during the past year and ensuing year to (a) the directors or persons performing similar functions, and (b) its officers and other persons, naming them wherever such remuneration exceeded $25,000 during any such year;

(15) the estimated net proceeds to be derived from the security to be offered;

(16) the price at which it is proposed that the security shall be offered to the public or the method by which such price is computed and any variation therefrom at which any portion of such security is proposed to be offered to any persons or classes of persons, other than the underwriters, naming them or specifying the class. A variation in price may be proposed prior to the date of the public offering of the security, but the Commission shall immediately be notified of such variation;

(17) all commissions or discounts paid or to be paid, directly or indirectly, by the issuer to the underwriters in respect of the sale of the security to be offered. Commissions shall include all cash, securities, contracts, or anything else of value, paid, to be set aside, disposed of, or understandings with or for the benefit of any other

persons in which any underwriter is interested, made, in connection with the sale of such security. A commission paid or to be paid in connection with the sale of such security by a person in which the issuer has an interest or which is controlled or directed by, or under common control with, the issuer shall be deemed to have been paid by the issuer. Where any such commission is paid the amount of such commission paid to each underwriter shall be stated;

(18) the amount or estimated amounts, itemized in reasonable detail, of expenses, other than commissions specified in paragraph (17) of this schedule, incurred or borne by or for the account of the issuer in connection with the sale of the security to be offered or properly chargeable thereto, including legal, engineering, certification, authentication, and other charges;

(19) the net proceeds derived from any security sold by the issuer during the two years preceding the filing of the registration statement, the price at which such security was offered to the public, and the names of the principal underwriters of such security;

(20) any amount paid within two years preceding the filing of the registration statement or intended to be paid to any promoter and the consideration for any such payment;

(21) the names and addresses of the vendors and the purchase price of any property, or good will, acquired or to be acquired, not in the ordinary course of business, which is to be defrayed in whole or in part from the proceeds of the security to be offered, the amount of any commission payable to any person in connection with such acquisition, and the name or names of such person or persons, together with any expense incurred or to be incurred in connection with such acquisition, including the cost of borrowing money to finance such acquisition;

(22) full particulars of the nature and extent of the interest, if any, of every director, principal executive officer, and of every stockholder holding more than 10 per centum of any class of stock or more than 10 per centum in the aggregate of the stock of the issuer, in any property acquired, not in the ordinary course of business of the issuer, within two years preceding the filing of the registration statement or proposed to be acquired at such date;

(23) the names and addresses of counsel who have passed on the legality of the issue;

(24) dates of and parties to, and the general effect concisely stated of every material contract made, not in the ordinary course of business, which contract is to be executed in whole or in part at or after the filing of the registration statement or which contract has been made not more than two years before such filing. Any management contract or contract providing for special bonuses or profit-sharing arrangements, and every material patent or contract for a material patent right, and every contract by or with a public utility company or an affiliate thereof, providing for the giving or receiving of technical or financial advice or service (if such contract may involve a charge to any party thereto at a rate in excess of $2,500 per year in cash or securities or anything else of value), shall be deemed a material contract;

(25) a balance sheet as of a date not more than ninety days prior to the date of the filing of the registration statement showing

all of the assets of the issuer, the nature and cost thereof, whenever determinable, in such detail and in such form as the Commission shall prescribe (with intangible items segregated), including any loan in excess of $20,000 to any officer, director, stockholder or person directly or indirectly controlling or controlled by the issuer, or person under direct or indirect common control with the issuer. All the liabilities of the issuer in such detail and such form as the Commission shall prescribe, including surplus of the issuer showing how and from what sources such surplus was created, all as of a date not more than ninety days prior to the filing of the registration statement. If such statement be not certified by an independent public or certified accountant, in addition to the balance sheet required to be submitted under this schedule, a similar detailed balance sheet of the assets and liabilities of the issuer, certified by an independent public or certified accountant, of a date not more than one year prior to the filing of the registration statement, shall be submitted;

(26) a profit and loss statement of the issuer showing earnings and income, the nature and source thereof, and the expenses and fixed charges in such detail and such form as the Commission shall prescribe for the latest fiscal year for which such statement is available and for the two preceding fiscal years, year by year, or, if such issuer has been in actual business for less than three years, then for such time as the issuer has been in actual business, year by year. If the date of the filing of the registration statement is more than six months after the close of the last fiscal year, a statement from such closing date to the latest practicable date. Such statement shall show what the practice of the issuer has been during the three years or lesser period as to the character of the charges, dividends or other distributions made against its various surplus accounts, and as to depreciation, depletion, and maintenance charges, in such detail and form as the Commission shall prescribe, and if stock dividends or avails from the sale of rights have been credited to income, they shall be shown separately with a statement of the basis upon which the credit is computed. Such statement shall also differentiate between any recurring and non-recurring income and between any investment and operating income. Such statement shall be certified by an independent public or certified accountant;

(27) if the proceeds, or any part of the proceeds, of the security to be issued is to be applied directly or indirectly to the purchase of any business, a profit and loss statement of such business certified by an independent public or certified accountant, meeting the requirements of paragraph (26) of this schedule, for the three preceding fiscal years, together with a balance sheet, similarly certified, of such business, meeting the requirements of paragraph (25) of this schedule of a date not more than ninety days prior to the filing of the registration statement or at the date such business was acquired by the issuer if the business was acquired by the issuer more than ninety days prior to the fiing of the registration statement;

(28) a copy of any agreement or agreements (or, if identical agreements are used, the forms thereof) made with any under-

writer, including all contracts and agreements referred to in paragraph (17) of this schedule;

(29) a copy of the opinion or opinions of counsel in respect to the legality of the issue, with a translation of such opinion, when necessary, into the English language;

(30) a copy of all material contracts referred to in paragraph (24) of this schedule, but no disclosure shall be required of any portion of any such contract if the Commission determines that disclosure of such portion would impair the value of the contract and would not be necessary for the protection of the investors;

(31) unless previously filed and registered under the provisions of this title, and brought up to date, (a) a copy of its articles of incorporation, with all amendments thereof and of its existing bylaws or instruments corresponding thereto, whatever the name, if the issuer be a corporation; (b) copy of all instruments by which the trust is created or declared, if the issuer is a trust; (c) a copy of its articles of partnership or association and all other papers pertaining to its organization, if the issuer is a partnership, unincorporated association, joint-stock company, or any other form of organization; and

(32) a copy of the underlying agreements or indentures affecting any stock, bonds, or debentures offered or to be offered.

In case of certificates of deposit, voting trust certificates, collateral trust certificates, certificates of interest or shares in unincorporated investment trusts, equipment trust certificates, interim or other receipts for certificates, and like securities, the Commission shall establish rules and regulations requiring the submission of information of a like character applicable to such cases, together with such other information as it may deem appropriate and necessary regarding the character, financial or otherwise, of the actual issuer of the securities and/or the person performing the acts and assuming the duties of depositor or manager.

SCHEDULE B

(1) Name of borrowing government or subdivision thereof;

(2) specific purposes in detail and the approximate amounts to be devoted to such purposes, so far as determinable, for which the security to be offered is to supply funds, and if the funds are to be raised in part from other sources, the amounts thereof and the sources thereof, shall be stated;

(3) the amount of the funded debt and the estimated amount of the floating debt outstanding and to be created by the security to be offered, excluding intergovernmental debt, and a brief description of the date, maturity, character of such debt, rate of interest, character of amortization provisions, and the security, if any, therefor. If substitution of any security is permissible, a statement of the conditions under which such substitution is permitted. If substitution is permissible without notice, a specific statement to that effect;

(4) whether or not the issuer or its predecessor has, within a period of twenty years prior to the filing of the registration statement, defaulted on the principal or interest of any external security, excluding intergovernmental debt, and, if so, the date,

amount, and circumstances of such default, and the terms of the succeeding arrangement, if any;

(5) the receipts, classified by source, and the expenditures, classified by purpose, in such detail and form as the Commission shall prescribe for the latest fiscal year for which such information is available and the two preceding fiscal years, year by year;

(6) the names and addresses of the underwriters;

(7) the name and address of its authorized agent, if any, in the United States;

(8) the estimated net proceeds to be derived from the sale in the United States of the security to be offered;

(9) the price at which it is proposed that the security shall be offered in the United States to the public or the method by which such price is computed. A variation in price may be proposed prior to the date of the public offering of the security, but the Commission shall immediately be notified of such variation;

(10) all commissions paid or to be paid, directly or indirectly, by the issuer to the underwriters in respect of the sale of the security to be offered. Commissions shall include all cash, securities, contracts, or anything else of value, paid, to be set aside, disposed of, or understandings with or for the benefit of any other persons in which the underwriter is interested, made, in connection with the sale of such security. Where any such commission is paid, the amount of such commission paid to each underwriter shall be stated;

(11) the amount or estimated amounts, itemized in reasonable detail, of expenses, other than the commission specified in paragraph (10) of this schedule, incurred or borne by or for the account of the issuer in connection with the sale of the security to be offered or properly chargeable thereto, including legal, engineering, certification, and other charges;

(12) the names and addresses of counsel who have passed upon the legality of the issue;

(13) a copy of any agreement or agreements made with any underwriter governing the sale of the security within the United States; and

(14) an agreement of the issuer to furnish a copy of the opinion or opinions of counsel in respect to the legality of the issue, with a translation, where necessary, into the English language. Such opinion shall set out in full all laws, decrees, ordinances, or other acts of Government under which the issue of such security has been authorized.

TITLE II

SEC. 201. [77bb] For the purpose of protecting, conserving, and advancing the interests of the holders of foreign securities in default, there is hereby created a body corporate with the name "Corporation of Foreign Security Holders" (herein called the "Corporation"). The principal office of the Corporation shall be located in the District of Columbia, but there may be established agencies or branch offices in any city or cities of the United States under rules and regulations prescribed by the board of directors.

SEC. 202. [77cc] The control and management of the Corporation shall be vested in a board of six directors, who shall be appointed and hold office in the following manner: As soon as practicable after the date this Act takes effect the Federal Trade Commission (hereinafter in this title called "Commission") shall appoint six directors, and shall designate a chairman and a vice chairman from among their number. After the directors designated as chairman and vice chairman cease to be directors, their successors as chairman and vice chairman shall be elected by the board of directors itself. Of the directors first appointed, two shall continue in office for a term of two years, two for a term of four years, and two for a term of six years, from the date of this Act takes effect, the term of each to be designated by the Commission at the time of appointment. Their successors shall be appointed by the Commission, each for a term of six years from the date of the expiration of the term for which his predecessor was appointed, except that any person appointed to fill a vacancy occurring prior to the expiration of the term for which his predecessor was appointed shall be appointed only for the unexpired term of such predecessor. No person shall be eligible to serve as a director who within the five years preceding has had any interest, direct or indirect, in any corporation, company, partnership, bank or association which has sold, or offered for sale any foreign securities. The office of a director shall be vacated if the board of directors shall at a meeting specially convened for that purpose by resolution passed by a majority of at least two thirds of the board of directors, remove such member from office, provided that the member whom it is proposed to remove shall have seven days' notice sent to him of such meeting and that he may be heard.

SEC. 203. [77dd] The Corporation shall have power to adopt, alter, and use a corporate seal; to make contracts; to lease such real estate as may be necessary for the transaction of its business; to sue and be sued, to complain and to defend, in any court of competent jurisdiction, State or Federal; to require from trustees, financial agents, or dealers in foreign securities information relative to the original or present holders of foreign securities and such other information as may be required and to issue subpenas therefor; to take over the functions of any fiscal and paying agents of any foreign securities in default; to borrow money for the purposes of this title, and to pledge as collateral for such loans any securities deposited with the Corporation pursuant to this title; by and with the consent and approval of the Commission to select, employ, and fix the compensation of officers, directors, members of committees, employees, attorneys, and agents of the Corporation, without regard to the provisions of other laws applicable to the employment and compensation of officers or employees of the United States; to define their authority and duties, require bonds of them and fix the penalties thereof, and to dismiss at pleasure such officers, employees, attorneys, and agents; and to prescribe, amend, and repeal, by its board of directors, bylaws, rules, and regulations governing the manner in which its general business may be conducted and the powers granted to it by law may be exercised and enjoyed, together with provisions for such committees and the functions thereof as the board of directors may deem necessary for facilitating its business under this title. The board of directors of the Corporation shall determine and prescribe the manner in which its obligations shall be incurred and its expenses allowed and paid.

SEC. 204. [77ee] The board of directors may—

(1) Convene meetings of holders of foreign securities.

(2) Invite the deposit and undertake the custody of foreign securities which have defaulted in the payment either of principal or interest, and issue receipts or certificates in the place of securities so deposited.

(3) Appoint committees from the directors of the Corporation and/or all other persons to represent holders of any class or classes of foreign securities which have defaulted in the payment either of principal or interest and determine and regulate the functions of such committees. The chairman and vice chairman of the board of directors shall be ex officio chairman and vice chairman of each committee.

(4) Negotiate and carry out, or assist in negotiating and carrying out, arrangements for the resumption of payments due or in arrears in respect of any foreign securities in default or for rearranging the terms on which such securities may in future be held or for converting and exchanging the same for new securities or for any other object in relation thereto; and under this paragraph any plan or agreement made with respect to such securities shall be binding upon depositors, providing that the consent of holders resident in the United States of 60 per centum of the securities deposited with the Corporation shall be obtained.

(5) Undertake, superintend, or take part in the collection and application of funds derived from foreign securities which come into the possession of or under the control or management of the Corporation.

(6) Collect, preserve, publish, circulate, and render available in readily accessible form, when deemed essential or necessary, documents, statistics, reports, and information of all kinds in respect of foreign securities, including particularly records of foreign external securities in default and records of the progress made toward the payment of past-due obligations.

(7) Take such steps as it may deem expedient with the view of securing the adoption of clear and simple forms of foreign securities and just and sound principles in the conditions and terms thereof.

(8) Generally, act in the name and on behalf of the holders of foreign securities the care or representation of whose interests may be entrusted to the Corporation; conserve and protect the rights and interests of holders of foreign securities issued, sold, or owned in the United States; adopt measures for the protection, vindication, and preservation or reservation of the rights and interests of holders of foreign securities either on any default in or on breach or contemplated breach of the conditions on which such foreign securities may have been issued, or otherwise; obtain for such holders such legal and other assistance and advice as the board of directors may deem expedient; and do all such other things as are incident or conducive to the attainment of the above objects.

SEC. 205. [77ff] The board of directors shall cause accounts to be kept of all matters relating to or connected with the transactions and business of the Corporation, and cause a general account and balance sheet of the Corporation to be made out in each year, and cause all accounts to be audited by one or more auditors who shall examine the same and report thereon to the board of directors.

SEC. 206. [77gg] The Corporation shall make, print, and make public an annual report of its operations during each year, send a copy thereof, together with a copy of the account and balance sheet and auditor's report, to the Commission and to both Houses of Congress, and provide one copy of such report but not more than one on the application of any person and on receipt of a sum not exceeding $1: *Provided,* That the board of directors in its discretion may distribute copies gratuitously.

SEC. 207. [77hh] The Corporation may in its discretion levy charges, assessed on a pro rata basis, on the holders of foreign securities deposited with it: *Provided,* That any charge levied at the time of depositing securities with the Corporation shall not exceed one fifth of 1 per centum of the face value of such securities: *Provided further,* That any additional charges shall bear a close relationship to the cost of operations and negotiations including those enumerated in sections 203 and 204 and shall not exceed 1 per centum of the face value of such securities.

SEC. 208. [77ii] The Corporation may receive subscriptions from any person, foundation with a public purpose, or agency of the United States Government, and such subscriptions may, in the discretion of the board of directors, be treated as loans repayable when and as the board of directors shall determine.

SEC. 209. [77jj] The Reconstruction Finance Corporation is hereby authorized to loan out of its funds not to exceed $75,000 for the use of the Corporation.

SEC. 210. [77kk] Notwithstanding the foregoing provisions of this title, it shall be unlawful for, and nothing in this title shall be taken or construed as permitting or authorizing, the Corporation in this title created, or any committee of said Corporation, or any person or persons acting for or representing or purporting to represent it—

    (a) to claim or assert or pretend to be acting for or to represent the Department of State or the United States Government;

    (b) to make any statements or representations of any kind to any foreign government or its officials or the officials of any political subdivision of any foreign government that said Corporation or any committee thereof or any individual or individuals connected therewith were speaking or acting for the said Department of State or the United States Government; or

    (c) to do any act directly or indirectly which would interfere with or obstruct or hinder or which might be calculated to obstruct, hinder or interfere with the policy or policies of the said Department of State or the Government of the United States or any pending or contemplated diplomatic negotiations, arrangements, business or exchanges between the Government of the United States or said Department of State and any foreign government or any political subdivision thereof.